PUBLIC DEBT IN A DEMOCRATIC SOCIETY

By James M. Buchanan *and* Richard E. Wagner

January, 1967

PUBLISHED AND DISTRIBUTED BY THE

AMERICAN ENTERPRISE INSTITUTE
FOR PUBLIC POLICY RESEARCH
WASHINGTON, D. C. 20036

———◆———

James M. Buchanan is Paul G. McIntire, Professor of Economics and Director of the Thomas Jefferson Center for Political Economy, University of Virginia. Richard E. Wagner is Assistant Professor of Economics at the University of California, Irvine.

———◆———

Price $1.00

AMERICAN ENTERPRISE INSTITUTE
For Public Policy Research

THE AMERICAN ENTERPRISE INSTITUTE FOR PUBLIC POLICY RE-
SEARCH, established in 1943, is a nonpartisan research and educa-
tional organization which studies national policy problems.

Institute publications take two major forms:

1. LEGISLATIVE AND SPECIAL ANALYSES—factual analyses of current legislative proposals and other public policy issues before
   the Congress prepared with the help of recognized experts in
   the academic world and in the fields of law and government.
   A typical analysis features: (1) pertinent background, (2) a
   digest of significant elements, and (3) a discussion, pro and
   con, of the issues. The reports reflect no policy position in
   favor of or against specific proposals.

2. LONG-RANGE STUDIES—basic studies of major national problems of significance for public policy. The Institute, with the
   counsel of its Advisory Board, utilizes the services of competent
   scholars, but the opinions expressed are those of the authors
   and represent no policy position on the part of the Institute.

CONTENTS

LIST OF TABLES

INTRODUCTION

Why should the average man be concerned about the public debt? Scholars have, on many occasions, taken great care to suggest that "we owe it to ourselves," or at least most of it. In addition, some economists say that the details of public debt are too complicated for the ordinary citizen to comprehend. On either or both of these grounds, should not the citizen shed off his worries and leave all problems of public debt to the expert wisdom of the economists and politicians?

Despite such advice, the public's concern over public debt has not subsided. Ordinary common sense suggests, and experience has shown, that the experts can make errors. When these errors seem likely to impose costs on the citizens, the ordinary man is probably wise when he tries to figure out for himself what the talk is all about. Why is the government so different from anything else? If one need not worry about public debt, what does this imply about private debt? Most private debts are also owed to fellow citizens, in one form or another; we also "owe this to ourselves." Either there must be some mysterious difference between public and private debt or at least some of the experts must be wrong. Too many persons know the consequences of following the private-debt siren to accept unwittingly the fiscal perpetual motion machine that sometimes seems to be offered by public debt.

Something more than the old-fashioned Puritan ethic, attributed to us all, makes the ordinary man wary of ever-increasing public debt. Deficits in the federal government's budget have come to be the order of events, and the public-debt totals creep ever upwards, seemingly despite the presence of prosperous, or even of inflationary, business

1

conditions. In late 1966, the national debt limit of $330 billion was beginning to inhibit Treasury action, and in early 1967, this limit should have been either raised or disregarded. State-local governments have also borrowed billions in postwar decades. Until he understands why he should not be, the citizen is properly concerned about public debts.

Democratic society depends on intelligent discussion and broad understanding of public issues by the citizenry. Professional scholars have a compelling obligation to present these issues clearly and forthrightly. This essay is presented with this purpose. For orderly discussion, facts are necessary, and the first part of the monograph presents these. Data on the growth, composition, and ownership of the national debt are summarized. But facts are less important than the clarification of ideas. Early in the discussion, some clarification must be aimed at the widespread confusion between public debt and money. Straight thinking about these two instruments leads to conclusions that differ radically from those based on the elementary confusion. Not surprisingly, policies that seem logical with confused thinking become quite illogical with straight thinking.

The second major part discusses the management of the national debt. This is important because the levels of prices, income, and employment can be affected by changes in debt-management policy.

The third part analyzes the controversial question about the burden of public debt. Here we ask: "Who sacrifices the goods and services necessary to provide the public services that are financed through the issue of public debt?" The elementary principles here are straightforward enough, but it is also necessary to examine and to refute the more complex and sometimes fallacious counter-arguments.

The fourth part treats important issues concerning the creation and retirement of public debt. When should governments borrow? When should public debt be retired?

The final chapter presents concluding comments that should be relevant for informed decision making by elected representatives as well as for more informed public discussion by the electorate.

NATIONAL DEBT

Definition

A public debt is an obligation of a governmental unit to make payments of specified amounts to holders of the debt instruments. National debt is an obligation of the national government in a federal political system. The government receives command over resources at the time the debt is undertaken in exchange for its promise to make future payments to the lenders. Ordinarily, these future payments allow for interest plus repayment of the principal. Only about 1 percent of the existing American national debt is noninterest-bearing. Also, though none exist in the United States, some securities, called consols, provide only for interest payments; no return of principal is involved.

It should be noted that the existing American national debt is a mixture of debt and money. Generally, the shorter the maturity date of a debt instrument, the greater its liquidity or "moneyness." A one-year government debt will be transformed automatically into money before a two-year debt. In this respect, debt instruments generally can be arrayed along a liquidity spectrum according to the time that must elapse before maturity. In the United States, national debt obligations range from 13 weeks to over 30 years from the initial borrowing to the time that the principal must be repaid. Consols are the ultimate or pure form of debt. Since the government is obligated to pay specified sums of interest in perpetuity without having to repay principal, they serve little liquidity or money-substitute purpose. They can be sold in a market transaction in exchange for money. Yet because they have less liquidity than any other debt instrument, they

4

form a benchmark in judging the relative liquidity of debt instruments. (Money is the other benchmark in judging relative liquidity; it is perfectly liquid. It is *not* public debt, however.)

Public debt is created through public borrowing. The government borrows funds for which it exchanges a promise to make future payments on terms mutually agreeable to both parties. Public debt represents a third means of financing public expenditures, the first two being taxation and money creation. Public debt is retired through repayment, the reverse process of debt creation. The government pays money to the holders in exchange for control over the debt instruments. The government may retire its debt by repurchasing its securities on the open market at the going price, or it may wait until maturity and retire them by paying off the principal.

The Distinction Between Debt Creation and Money Creation

Debt creation and money creation are often used synonymously in discussions of public policy, with much analytical confusion. Many inferences, based on the equivalence of debt and money, often break down when their fundamental distinctiveness is recognized. *Public debt creation involves an exchange of purchasing power* between the borrower (the government) and the lender (any individual or firm that buys government securities). By contrast, *money creation involves no such exchange,* it is simply a creation of new purchasing power.

Existing monetary and debt institutions contribute to the confusion between debt and money. Within the context of a fixed national debt, the money supply increases with Federal Reserve purchases of national debt from the public and decreases with Federal Reserve sales of national debt to the public. A similar confusion exists when national debt is expanded through budget deficits. The now-orthodox fiscal policy prescription is for the government to run a budget deficit when the economy is not at potential GNP. But a deficit may not be expansionary if the debt is sold to private individuals. Instead there may be simply a transfer of purchasing power from individuals to the government. If the debt is sold to the Federal Reserve, however, the effect will be expansionary because multiple expansion of the money supply will result from the creation of bank reserves. *But the beneficial impact of financing the deficit through such debt issue lies in its monetary properties, not in its debt properties.* If pure debt should be issued, which happens when the debt is sold to non-bank holders, the budget deficit may not be expansive. The deficit becomes directly stimulating to the economy only as it is sold to the banking systems, providing an additional reserve base for an expansion of the money supply. This amounts to saying that such debt issue is stimulating only to the extent that it represents disguised money creation.

In contrast to common folklore, public debt issue is deflationary, not inflationary. An individual who purchases public debt gives up current purchasing power in exchange for a greater amount of future purchasing power. Debt issue reduces private spending. The sale of debt instruments to the Federal Reserve System leads to an expansionary multiple increase in the money supply, but the expansion results from disguised money creation and could be accomplished without the issue of national debt.

This confusion between debt and money, and the means of their creation, is found throughout the post-Keynesian literature on countercyclical economic policy. Traditional fiscal norms such as a balanced government budget have been criticized because public debt issue could occur only under prespecified conditions and the beneficial effects of deficit spending could not be realized. Interestingly, however, these benefits may not exist even with debt financing if bonds are sold to private citizens. The deficit is certain to be expansionary only if debt instruments are "sold" to the Federal Reserve System. *Yet public debt need not be increased to increase the money supply through budget deficits.* In fact, it is probably the existing confusion between debt and money that allows interest to be paid on monetary expansion—a wholly unnecessary cost—without undue complaint. As an alternative, budget deficits could be financed directly through money creation. Under this alternative, public debt is not issued, and the additional interest payments (and the taxes necessary to finance them) do not arise.

When the common confusion between debt and money creation is appreciated, it becomes evident that changes in the quantity of national debt are logically unrelated to countercyclical policies.

Growth of the National Debt

Table 1 shows the growth of the American national debt, measured by its maturity value, for selected years since 1860. Both the growth of the principal value and the relation between debt and Gross National Product (GNP) prompt interesting observations.

Until the depression of the 1930s, increases in national debt were associated predominantly with national warfare. Also, until the depression, a conscious public policy of debt retirement seems to have

6

Table 1

National Debt and the Ratio of National Debt to GNP, Selected Years, 1860 to 1965
(fiscal years ending June 30)

Year	National Debt (principal value in billions of dollars) (1)	National Debt as a Percentage of GNP[a] (2)
1860	$ 0.07	1.2
1865	2.68	45.3
1870	2.44	37.5
1880	2.09	21.8
1890	1.12	9.0
1900	1.26	6.8
1910	1.15	3.5
1916	1.23	2.4
1919	25.49	32.3
1920	24.30	27.3
1930	16.19	17.9
1940	42.97	43.1
1945	258.68	122.0
1946	269.42	129.2
1947	258.29	111.7
1948	252.29	97.9
1949	252.77	98.5
1950	257.36	90.4
1951	255.22	77.7
1952	259.11	75.0
1953	266.07	72.9
1954	271.26	74.4
1955	274.37	68.9
1956	272.75	65.1
1957	270.53	61.3
1958	276.34	61.8
1959	284.71	58.9
1960	286.33	56.7
1961	288.97	55.6
1962	298.20	53.2
1963	305.86	51.9
1964	311.71	49.6
1965	317.27	47.0

[a] The GNP figures from 1870 through 1916 are estimated from figures showing five year averages over that period. No figures appear prior to 1870, so GNP for 1860 and 1865 was estimated by extending the five year averages back through time. Although this involves some error, it should not be too serious because of the relatively short time period involved.

SOURCES: Column 1: *Annual Report of the Secretary of the Treasury, 1964* (Washington: U.S. Government Printing Office, 1965), pp. 460-61, for the

6

existed. Column 1 provides evidence for both of these statements. The national debt was $65 million in 1860, but five years of civil warfare pushed it to $2.7 billion. National debt was reduced to the vicinity of $1.1 billion by 1890 where it remained until 1916. By 1919, at the conclusion of World War I, the national debt had soared some twentyfold to $25.5 billion. By 1930, after another conscious effort at debt reduction, it was $16.2 billion. The Great Depression destroyed government budget balancing, leaving a $43 billion debt in 1940. Under the stimulus of World War II, the national debt raced to $258.7 billion by 1945. Since 1945 the national debt has grown at about $3 billion per year, indicating the final demise, begun in the 1930s, of a conscious debt retirement policy.

The figures in column 2 show the ratio of national debt to GNP. Throughout most of the pre-1930 period, the ratio was less than 20 percent. After the Civil War and World War I, it stood at nearly one half and one third respectively, but subsequently declined to lower levels. The combination of depression and World War II raised the ratio to about 125 percent in 1945. Since then, despite the gradual increase in the absolute amount of debt, the ratio to GNP has again been declining and, in 1965, was less than 50 percent.

Composition of the National Debt

The national debt is made up basically of bills, notes, and bonds, with the distinction between these being primarily in terms of their maturity schedules. Treasury bills usually have 13 or 26 week maturities, although there are some one-year issues. Treasury notes range from one to five years in maturities, and bonds are issued for longer periods. Table 2 shows the composition of the national debt as of January 30, 1966. Distinction should also be made between marketable and nonmarketable debt. As Table 2 shows, over two thirds of the national debt is marketable. U.S. Savings Bonds are the largest class of nonmarketable debt; an individual holder may not sell his savings bonds to someone else at a mutually agreeable price; he must either hold these until maturity or sell them to the federal government at a price stipulated previously. A final, important, cate-

years through 1964. The 1965 figure comes from the *Treasury Bulletin,* July, 1965, p. 21. Column 2: Entries in column 1 are divided by the corresponding figure for GNP. The GNP figures for 1860 through 1920 are derived from the Census Bureau's *Historical Statistics of the United States* (Washington: U.S. Government Printing Office, 1960), Series F-1, p. 139. The 1930 through 1965 figures are taken from the *Economic Report of the President, 1966* (Washington: U.S. Government Printing Office, 1966), p. 209.

Table 2

Composition of the National Debt, January 30, 1966
(millions of dollars)

Type of Debt	Marketable	Nonmarketable
Bills	$ 61,589	
Certificates	1,652	$ 1,099[a]
Notes	50,244	
Bonds		
Treasury Bonds	104,171	2,780
U.S. Savings Bonds		50,319
Foreign Currency Bonds		1,207[b]
Depository Bonds		47
Other Bonds		135
Special Issues		44,356
Non-interest Bearing		4,404
Total	$217,656	$104,347
Total National Debt		$322,003

[a] These are the Foreign Series issues (debts sold to foreigners but payable in dollars). They include $615 million in certificates, $310 million in notes, and $174 million in bonds.

[b] The Foreign Currency Series issues are payable in foreign currencies. This amount includes $912 million in bonds and $295 million in certificates.

SOURCE: *Treasury Bulletin,* February, 1966, p. 27.

gory of national debt is the special issues, often called intragovernmental debt. Special issues arise whenever agencies of the federal government hold national debt for a reserve. For example, the Federal Old-Age and Survivors Insurance Trust Fund holds about $18 billion of national debt and the Civil Service Retirement and Disability Fund holds nearly $15 billion.

Although changes occur in the composition of the national debt over time, the annual changes are small and the prevailing composition seems likely to persist over the next several years. Table 3 shows the composition of the national debt by both percentage of total debt and actual magnitudes for the ten-year period 1956-65. Note that changes in composition have occurred over this decade but these have been relatively moderate. Marketable issues have increased from 57 percent to 66 percent of total national debt; marketable Treasury bills more than doubled their share; and certificates of indebtedness have practically disappeared. Yet the gradualness of the changes gives reason to believe that the composition of the national debt will not be altered greatly over the late 1960s and early 1970s. Although the actual magnitudes of Table 2 will be outdated quickly as national debt continues to grow, the underlying percentages will change more slowly. Table 3 should be a useful indicator of the composition of the national debt for several years.

Ownership of the National Debt

The ownership of the national debt has important implications for estimating the potential effect of national debt on the economy. Table 4, which shows the ownership of the national debt on December 30, 1965, indicates that the national debt is owned primarily by Federal Reserve banks, commercial banks, individuals, U.S. government agencies, corporations, and state and local governments. The distinction between bank-held and non-bank-held debt is the most important distinction to make in estimating the potential effect of national debt on the economy. Also, the distribution of newly created national debt among these classes of ownership has significant implications for future levels of economic activity.

The existing pattern of ownership of the national debt can affect future levels of economic activity in several ways. The amount of debt held by commercial banks indicates the potential scope for increases in reserves through the sale by them of Treasury debt. The distribution of national debt between the Federal Reserve System and other units in the economy indicates the room that exists for open-market operations. A Federal Reserve purchase of bonds from individuals, for instance, can cause a multiple expansion of the money supply. Finally, the amount of national debt held outside of the banking system indicates the potential scope for increases in the money supply through a policy of debt monetization (this is discussed below, pp. 52-53).

With respect to the distribution of newly created debt among the various classes of ownership, increases in non-bank-held debt have no potential effects. It makes no difference if the debt is held by individuals, corporations, insurance companies, or local governments. Treasury sales of national debt to these units for financing government expenditures affect neither the money supply nor bank reserves. If an individual purchases a Treasury bond, purchasing power is transferred from the individual to the government, and with the expenditure of the funds by the government, the money supply, which influences the total level of economic activity, is unaffected. The

Table 3[a]

Composition of the National Debt, 1956-65, for Fiscal Years Ending June 30

(billions of dollars)

Year	Total Debt (1)	Marketable					Total Non-marketable (7)	Nonmarketable		
		Total Marketable (2)	Bills (3)	Certificates (4)	Notes (5)	Bonds (6)		Public Issues[b] (8)	Special Issues (9)	Noninterest-Bearing (10)
1956	272.8	155.0 (56.8)	20.8 (7.6)	16.3 (6.0)	36.0 (13.2)	81.9 (30.0)	117.8 (43.2)	69.8 (25.6)	45.1 (16.5)	2.9 (1.1)
1957	270.5	155.7 (57.6)	23.4 (8.7)	20.5 (7.6)	31.0 (11.5)	80.8 (29.9)	114.8 (42.4)	66.0 (24.4)	46.8 (17.3)	2.0 (0.7)
1958	276.3	166.7 (60.3)	22.4 (8.1)	32.9 (11.9)	20.4 (7.4)	90.9 (32.9)	109.6 (39.7)	61.8 (22.4)	46.2 (16.7)	1.6 (0.6)
1959	284.7	178.0 (62.5)	32.0 (11.2)	33.8 (11.9)	27.3 (9.6)	84.9 (29.8)	106.7 (37.5)	59.1 (20.8)	44.8 (15.7)	2.8 (1.0)
1960	286.3	183.8 (64.2)	33.4 (11.7)	17.7 (6.2)	51.5 (18.0)	81.3 (28.4)	102.5 (35.8)	54.5 (19.0)	44.9 (15.7)	3.1 (1.1)
1961	289.0	187.1 (64.7)	36.7 (12.7)	13.3 (4.6)	56.3 (19.5)	80.8 (27.9)	101.9 (35.3)	53.5 (18.5)	45.0 (15.6)	3.4 (1.2)
1962	298.2	196.1 (65.8)	42.0 (14.1)	13.5 (4.5)	65.5 (22.0)	75.0 (25.2)	102.1 (34.2)	53.4 (17.9)	44.9 (15.1)	3.8 (1.3)
1963	305.9	203.5 (66.5)	47.2 (15.4)	22.2 (7.3)	52.1 (17.0)	82.0 (26.8)	102.4 (33.5)	53.6 (17.5)	44.8 (14.6)	4.0 (1.3)
1964	311.7	206.5 (66.2)	50.7 (16.3)	----	67.3 (21.6)	88.5 (28.4)	105.2 (33.8)	54.2 (17.4)	46.6 (15.0)	4.4 (1.4)
1965	317.3	208.7 (65.8)	53.7 (16.9)	----	52.5 (16.5)	102.5 (32.3)	108.6 (34.2)	55.8 (17.6)	48.7 (15.3)	4.2 (1.3)

[a] Figures in parentheses indicate percentages of total national debt.
[b] These issues consist primarily of U.S. Savings Bonds, Treasury Investment Bonds, and Foreign Series and Foreign Currency Series issues.

SOURCE: *Annual Report of the Secretary of the Treasury 1964*, pp. 463-65; *Treasury Bulletin*, July, 1965, p. 22.

Table 4

Ownership of the National Debt, December 30, 1965
(billions of dollars)

Owner	Amount Owned
Commercial Banks	$ 60.9
Federal Reserve Banks	40.8
U.S. Government Investment Accounts	61.9
Individuals	72.2
Insurance Companies	10.4
Mutual Savings Banks	5.4
Corporations	15.7
State and Local Governments	22.9
Foreign and International	16.5
Other Owners	14.7
Total	$321.4

SOURCE: *Treasury Bulletin,* February, 1966, p. 72.

sale of Treasury bonds to commercial banks, coupled with subsequent government spending of the funds secured, increases the money supply, but decreases excess reserves by the same amount. This situation is expansionary only to the extent that excess reserves exist. The sale of Treasury bonds to the Federal Reserve System, coupled with the subsequent government spending, entails a multiple expansion of the money supply. If the reserve requirement is 16⅔ percent, then the potential expansion of the money supply is six times the amount of the bond sale.

Table 5 shows both the percentage distribution and the actual magnitudes of the ownership of the national debt over the ten years 1956-65. As shown there, few significant changes in the distribution of ownership occurred. With regard to ownership changes, it is especially interesting to note cyclical changes in the distribution of ownership between commercial banks and the Federal Reserve System. The sale of debt by commercial banks to the Federal Reserve System indicates monetary expansion. In this light, between 1962 and 1965, commercial bank holdings of national debt decreased by nearly $10 billion while Federal Reserve holdings increased by roughly the same amount. Also, the period, 1962-65, is unique in the ten-year period in that the Federal Reserve System increased its proportion of total national debt held. In general, changes in ownership have been gradual, and it seems likely that the basic ownership pattern will continue to exist in the near future although the particular numerical magnitudes will change.

Table 5[a]

Ownership of the National Debt, 1956-65, for Fiscal Years Ending June 30
(billions of dollars)

Year	Commercial Banks (1)	Federal Reserve Banks (2)	U.S. Gov't Investment Accounts (3)	Individuals (4)	Insurance Companies (5)	Mutual Savings Banks (6)	Corporations (7)	State and Local Government (8)	Foreign and International (9)	Other Owners[b] (10)
1956	57.3 (21.0)	23.8 (8.7)	53.5 (19.6)	138.3 (50.7)	13.6 (5.0)	8.4 (3.1)	17.3 (6.3)	16.1 (5.9)	7.9 (2.9)	8.4 (3.1)
1957	56.2 (20.8)	23.0 (8.5)	55.6 (20.5)	135.9 (50.2)	12.7 (4.7)	7.9 (2.9)	16.1 (5.9)	16.8 (6.2)	7.6 (2.8)	8.4 (3.1)
1958	65.3 (23.6)	25.4 (9.2)	55.9 (20.2)	129.9 (47.0)	12.2 (4.4)	7.4 (2.7)	14.1 (5.1)	16.3 (5.9)	6.5 (2.4)	8.8 (3.2)
1959	61.5 (21.6)	26.0 (9.1)	54.6 (19.2)	142.6 (50.1)	12.6 (4.4)	7.3 (2.6)	19.8 (7.0)	16.9 (5.9)	10.1 (3.5)	9.5 (3.3)
1960	55.3 (19.3)	26.5 (9.2)	55.3 (19.3)	149.3 (52.1)	12.0 (4.2)	6.6 (2.3)	19.5 (6.8)	18.8 (6.6)	12.3 (4.3)	10.4 (3.6)
1961	62.5 (21.6)	27.3 (9.4)	56.1 (19.4)	143.3 (49.6)	11.4 (3.9)	6.3 (2.2)	18.5 (6.4)	19.3 (6.7)	12.7 (4.4)	10.5 (3.6)
1962	65.2 (21.8)	29.7 (9.9)	56.5 (18.9)	147.3 (49.3)	11.4 (3.8)	6.3 (2.1)	18.2 (6.1)	20.1 (6.7)	14.1 (4.7)	11.6 (3.9)
1963	64.4 (21.0)	32.0 (10.4)	58.4 (19.1)	151.7 (49.5)	11.0 (3.6)	6.1 (2.0)	18.7 (6.1)	21.5 (7.0)	15.8 (5.2)	12.5 (4.1)
1964	60.2 (19.3)	34.8 (11.1)	61.1 (19.6)	156.4 (50.0)	10.9 (3.5)	6.0 (1.9)	18.5 (5.9)	22.5 (7.2)	15.6 (5.0)	13.7 (4.4)
1965	57.9 (18.2)	39.1 (12.3)	63.4 (19.9)	157.5 (49.5)	10.6 (3.3)	5.8 (1.8)	15.9 (5.0)	23.6 (7.4)	15.7 (4.9)	14.8 (4.7)

[a] Figures in parentheses indicate percentage of total national dept.
[b] Includes savings and loan associations, nonprofit institutions, corporate pension trust funds, and dealers and brokers.
SOURCE: *Treasury Bulletin*, September, 1965, p. 66.

analyze the controversial question about the burden of the public debt and ask: "Who sacrifices the goods and services necessary to provide the public services that are financed through the issue of public debt?" Is there a burden to the public debt and, if so, when does the burden occur? The elementary principles are straightforward enough, they state, but it is also necessary to examine and refute the more complex and sometimes fallacious counter-arguments.

The study deals with important issues concerning the creation and retirement of public debt, including questions of when governments should borrow and when public debt should be repaid.

The authors conclude that a deliberate policy of systematic repayment of national debt from tax-financed budgetary surpluses seems beyond the realm of current political plausibility. They predict that at the national level the U.S. will probably continue to experience budget deficits more or less continuously as it has over the postwar years. This means a gradual increase in both the nominal size of the national debt and in the real obligation that the debt represents.

———◆———

James M. Buchanan is Paul G. McIntire Professor of Economics and Director of the Thomas Jefferson Center for Political Economy, University of Virginia.

Richard E. Wagner is Assistant Professor of Economics at the University of California, Irvine.

PUBLIC DEBT
IN A DEMOCRATIC SOCIETY

By James M. Buchanan and Richard E. Wagner

The national debt rose by some $40 billion from the end of 1960 till the end of 1966. In late 1966 the national debt limit of $330 billion was inhibiting Treasury action with the clear implication that the ceiling would have to be raised in early 1967. Also, state and local governments have been increasing their indebtedness rapidly. This constantly mounting level of government debt deeply concerns many people.

In *Public Debt in a Democratic Society,* Professors Buchanan and Wagner have presented some of the public issues involved in the growth of public debt. While they have summarized the growth, composition, and ownership of the national debt, the authors are mainly concerned with the clarification of ideas. Thus, early in the study they discuss the relation between public debt and money—a subject of widespread confusion. As the authors state:

> Debt creation and money creation are often used synonymously in discussions of public policy, with much analytical confusion. Many inferences, based on the equivalence of debt and money, often break down when their fundamental distinctiveness is recognized.

The authors note that this confusion between money and debt and the means of their creation is found throughout the post-Keynesian literature on countercyclical economic policy.

> . . . Public debt creation involves an exchange of purchasing power between the borrower (the government) and the lender (any individual or firm that buys government securities). By contrast, money creation involves no such exchange, it is simply a creation of new purchasing power.

Professors Buchanan and Wagner discuss the management of the national debt, important because the levels of prices, income, and employment can be affected by changes in debt management policy. They

NATIONAL DEBT MANAGEMENT

The Debt Management Problem

In late 1966 the national debt was approaching $330 billion. Problems of managing this debt would exist even in a regime of budget balance, that is, even if no new debt were created. Debt management problems arise because issues of existing debt continually mature, and the Treasury must find some means of refinancing. The debt is more-or-less permanent as a whole, but individual debt instruments have definite maturity dates. The use of temporary debt instruments to finance a permanent debt requires that the temporary instruments be refinanced when they become due. A substantial part of the national debt is refinanced each year; some of it (bills) more than once. This need for refinancing constitutes the debt management problem. Budget deficits add to the magnitude of the problem by enlarging the debt, but do not affect the need for continual refinancing. Since debt management is a complicated, technical operation that requires great effort, means of reducing the problem are sought.

Debt retirement is one obvious means of reducing the management task. Any reduction in the size of the national debt clearly reduces the effort that must be spent in refunding existing debt because the existing debt becomes smaller. It seems safe to say, however, that the debt management problem will not be reduced in this fashion. On the contrary, since budget deficits seem to have become the usual state of affairs, the debt management problem is likely to increase through deficit-induced increases in the national debt.

Within the framework of an unchanged national debt, debt monetization can reduce the debt management problem. The money supply

13

14

could be expanded through time, in line with increases in national productivity, by Federal Reserve purchases of national debt on the open market. Although the principal value of the debt would be unchanged because of the peculiar use of debt to expand the money supply, the management problem would be reduced in proportion to the relative increase in Federal Reserve holdings of national debt. Since the Federal Reserve System is an arm of national monetary policy, no management problem need exist with respect to the national debt that it holds. Only the national debt held outside of the Federal Reserve System, which would be declining, creates a management problem.

The debt management problem can also be reduced by lengthening the maturity structure of the national debt. With an average maturity structure of five years, the entire value of the debt is refunded in five years. If the average maturity increases to ten years, 10 percent, instead of 20 percent, rolls over each year. Consols are the ultimate form of debt lengthening. Since they are issued in perpetuity, the debt management problem vanishes with their use.

On a somewhat different level of consideration, changes in techniques of debt management can reduce the management problem.[1] Suggested alternative management techniques are concerned primarily with increasing the use of routine procedures for refunding. This has been largely achieved for Treasury bills which turn over on 13 and 26 week bases. Suggestions for more routine handling of notes and bonds include regular scheduling of sales, and of achieving a more even flow of debt toward maturity. Presently, the Treasury enters the long-term market at irregular, unscheduled intervals. This reduces its market because previous commitments of funds prevent many potential investors, who try to keep slack funds at a minimum, from purchasing debt instruments. They would probably purchase Treasury debt if regularly scheduled sales dates enabled them to work these into their calendar of operations. Furthermore, some issues of Treasury debt are much larger than others. Use of more routine procedures would be facilitated if all issues were about the same size. At the same time, it should be pointed out that the Treasury frequently attempts to accommodate its debt issue to the needs of institutional investors in order to lighten its refunding burden.

[1] See Tilford C. Gaines, *Techniques of Treasury Debt Management* (Glencoe: The Free Press, 1962), esp. pp. 276-96, for a discussion of some alternative management techniques. This book is a good discussion of many aspects of debt management.

One apparently successful innovation in debt management was introduced in the early 1960s. This involves the advanced refunding of maturing issues of national debt. Holders of debt instruments that are scheduled to mature in the near future are offered opportunities to replace these securities in their portfolios with new issues carrying especially favorable terms. In this way, the whole refunding operation becomes more systematic, both for the Treasury and for the investor.

Objectives of Debt Management

Funding. One of several possible objectives of debt management policy is funding, the lengthening of the debt structure. The funding objective attempts to reduce the management problem by reducing the rate at which the national debt turns over. Since interest rates normally rise as the length to maturity increases, successful pursuit of this objective will increase interest payments. For example, if an increase in average maturity entails a rise in the interest rate from 3 to 4 percent with a $300 billion national debt, interest charges rise from $9 billion to $12 billion. Public revenues which could be used for alternative public projects are diverted to additional interest payment if a policy of funding is successful.[2]

Minimization of Interest Cost. A substantial portion of the federal budget is devoted to paying interest on the national debt. If interest charges could be reduced, desired additions to public spending could be made or tax rates decreased. This simple fact suggests that the minimization of interest cost is one objective for debt management.

As the maturity of debt is reduced, interest rates normally tend to be reduced. In the extreme case, debt instruments with near-zero maturity could be issued, with little, if any, interest charge. Such instruments would be almost equivalent to money, which, of course, bears no interest. If the minimization of interest cost should be the only objective for management, the Treasury could accomplish this readily by effectively monetizing the whole of the national debt. That it does not do so suggests that the cost minimization objective may be dominant for small changes in management policy, but that there is general recognition that wholesale pursuing of this objective would not be feasible.

Coordination With Macroeconomic Policy. Debt management can affect the level of economic activity, through its potential for modify-

[2] See Appendix 2 for a brief analysis of the relation between maturity structure of the debt and the level of interest charges.

ing the net liquidity in the economy. If the maturity structure of the debt is shortened, the debt instruments represent more liquidity for their holders. This increased liquidity tends to stimulate the rate of spending; the velocity of money increases. Lengthening the maturity structure will have the opposite effect; liquidity in the economy is reduced, and spending will tend to fall.

Because it does exert these effects, one plausible objective for debt management is surely that of coordination with the monetary-fiscal policies that are undertaken by Federal Reserve and other governmental agencies. If total demand is deficient, overall policy should be expansive. The supply of money should be increased, and injected into the system either through deficits or through open-market operations of the Federal Reserve authorities. Debt management can assist in these efforts only if, during this period, maturing issues are refunded with issues containing additional liquidity, that is, if the maturity structure is shortened.

If total demand is excessive, if inflation threatens, macroeconomic policy should be restrictive. Debt management in such a period should assist in reducing liquidity in the system if this objective is dominant. Maturing issues of bills should, for example, be refunded with long-term bonds.

This policy of coordination would increase interest costs on the national debt rather than to lower them, and it stands, therefore, in direct conflict with the cost-minimization objective. The policy of coordination amounts to "buying dear and selling cheap." The Treasury would have to enter the long-term market when rates are high, and leave it when rates are low.

Globally considered, this policy objective has much in its favor. Institutional factors create difficulties with its implementation, however, and these may be important. The Federal Reserve Board, empowered to carry out monetary policy independently, is not an arm of the Treasury, which must carry out debt management operations. Genuine coordination would require much closer cooperation between these two agencies than has existed in the past, and there are strong arguments against deliberate institutional changes that would make such cooperation effective.

Neutrality. Another possible goal or objective for debt management is that of maintaining neutrality in its effects on economic activity. Here policy would be aimed at maintaining a relatively stable liquidity element in the national debt, a relatively constant degree of "moneyness." To this end, a relatively stable maturity structure might be indicated. Explicit attempts at coordination with macroeconomic policy would be avoided.

Strong arguments can be advanced for this objective. At best, coordination would be of relatively minor assistance, and any attempt at coordination creates uncertainties that can be eliminated with a neutral policy.

Mutual Conflict Among Debt Management Objectives. The several possible objectives for debt management policy are not mutually consistent. Some compromise must be found. Cost minimization conflicts perhaps most clearly with other objectives. Funding, on balance, tends to increase not to decrease interest costs, and a coordination policy tends to increase costs during periods of excessive demand. Funding conflicts with the neutrality objective, and both of these conflict with a policy of coordination. Consideration of the conflicts among objectives provides one argument for a neutral policy, since, as an objective, neutrality tends to achieve perhaps the best balance.

Management Policies in the Postwar Period

Debt management policies since 1946 fall nicely into two periods, from 1946 to 1951 and from 1952 to the present. In terms of the objectives of debt management policy, the minimization of costs seems to have been paramount in both eras. The major difference is that in the former period the policy was pursued more openly than in the latter. That cost minimization is probably the major objective in the post-1951 period is revealed only by an examination of the national debt structure.

During World War II, commercial banks accumulated large amounts of government debt. They were encouraged to do so by explicit policy on the part of Federal Reserve authorities. After the war, the commercial banks sought to unload some of their government debt in order to provide a reserve base for an expansion of loans; the cessation of hostilities opened up many opportunities for private investment. Commercial banks desired to unload some of their government debt to take advantage of the more profitable private uses of funds.

On the other hand, the Treasury wanted to continue borrowing at the low wartime interest rates. If the Treasury should have been forced to compete with other demanders of funds, it might have found it necessary to pay much higher interest rates. Had the banks been allowed to sell some of their government securities the price of bonds would have been reduced—interest rates generally would have been increased. To compete for funds in the open market, the Treasury would have had to offer higher rates; greater payments to bondholders would have been required to acquire command over funds.

Two alternatives were open: the Treasury could adjust to a free market, paying whatever interest rates might be necessary, or it could devise a means of circumventing the market-dictated higher interest rates. The latter was chosen as national policy in the 1946-51 period. There is but one buyer for Treasury bonds at below-market interest rates—the Federal Reserve System. The Federal Reserve-Treasury policy dictated that Treasury bonds should not fall below par values, which is to say that interest rates should not rise above their announced levels. The Federal Reserve System became the major buyer of Treasury bonds over this period. It bought whatever quantity was necessary to maintain the above-market bond prices. As every student of elementary economics learns, Federal Reserve bond purchases provide bases for multiple expansions in the money supply. This is exactly what happened in the immediate postwar years, and this, when combined with strong demand, led to the inflation of 1946-48 and again that of 1950-51.

The untenability of the bond price support policy became apparent. Finally, in March, 1951, the Treasury and the Federal Reserve reached their now famous "accord." The accord was simply an agreement between the Treasury and the Federal Reserve that the latter would no longer support government bond prices.

The post-accord period signals a new look in debt management policy. No longer was the Treasury insulated from the operation of market forces. Yet exposure did not come abruptly. Conscious effort was undertaken by the Treasury and the Federal Reserve to make the transition to a free market gradual. The Federal Reserve agreed not to raise its discount rate, and gave some support to the Treasury bond market. With Federal Reserve support of the government market, the fall in bond prices was slow and gradual rather than rapid and abrupt as would be suggested by the operation of market forces on the significantly over-priced government bonds. The transition was probably finished by 1953.

With the accord, an announced policy of interest minimization ceased. Before the accord the Treasury used the Federal Reserve to keep interest costs low, but since then the Federal Reserve has been free to pursue whatever policies it sees fit. Post-accord Treasury debt management policies have lacked this institutional assistance of the Federal Reserve System but these have still been keyed to maintaining low interest costs, as an examination of recent debt management history seems to show.

On June 30, 1954, the average maturity of the national debt was five years and six months. Economic activity surged upward over the next three years. The average maturity length fell to four years and nine months by June 30, 1957. Such a policy resulted from the desire to seek lower interest rates; the Treasury did not desire to borrow in the long-term market when interest rates were rising. During this period, the Moody's Aaa interest rate rose by one third, going from 2.90 percent to 3.89 percent.

The economy fell into a recession during 1957 and 1958. A co-ordinated policy would have called for debt shortening. Yet the average maturity value rose from four years and nine months to five years and three months. The direct stimulus came from the desire to take advantage of the low long-term interest rates. Over this period, the Moody's Aaa rate on corporate bonds fell from 3.89 percent to 3.79 percent. This is in sharp contrast to the one-third rise over the preceding three years—and the recessionary debt management policy contrasted sharply with the policy of the preceding three years.

The economy again moved upward from 1958 to 1960. In line with the revived state of economic affairs, long-term interest rates returned to their upward trek. From a 1958 trough of 3.79 percent, they stood at 4.41 percent as of June 30, 1960. This rise of 20 percent coincided with a shortening of the average national debt from five years and three months to four years and four months. Again the desire for lower interest costs seemed to dominate the Treasury's debt management policy.

As former Vice President Nixon will undoubtedly long remember, the economy, never buoyant after the 1957-58 recession, hit a snag in 1960 that ran through the election and into 1961. The Moody's Aaa interest rate fell from 4.41 percent to 4.35 percent. Again the Treasury responded by lengthening the average maturity date from four years and four months to four years and six months. The years immediately following were years of recovery and expansion under the stimulus of an easy money policy and budget deficits. Moody's Aaa rates continued to fall, partially due to a government attempt to keep long-term interest rates low, going from 4.35 percent in 1961 to 4.33 percent in 1962 and 4.26 percent in 1963. Quite predictably, the Treasury responded by lengthening its maturity structure from four years and six months in 1961 to five years and one month in 1963. Again the search for lower interest rates seemed to dominate debt management policy. In fact, this conflicted directly with an official policy of reducing long-term rates relative to short-term rates. This policy would require a shortening of the debt structure; a decreased supply of long-term bonds increases their price, which means a fall in their interest rate.

Treasury actions between 1963 and 1965 did not seem to be keyed to reducing interest costs. Moody's Aaa interest rates rose from 4.26 percent in 1963 to 4.40 percent in 1964 and 4.49 percent in 1965. The average maturity of five years and one month in 1963 fell to five years in 1964 and then rose to five years and four months in 1965. This seems to indicate the lack of an attempt to shorten the maturity structure because of the rising long-term interest rates. The one-month fall in the maturity structure between 1963 and 1964 does not indicate a significant response to the rising interest rate. Furthermore, the maturity structure rose four months between 1964 and 1965 in the face of a slight rise in long-term interest rates.

Events after the beginning of the new fiscal year on July 1, 1965, suggest that the behavior of debt management policy over the 1964-65 fiscal year was but an interlude in the struggle for lower interest rates on the national debt. Fiscal 1966 was characterized by concern over the possibility of inflation. During this period interest rates continued to rise. The average maturity structure of the national debt dropped from five years and four months on June 30, 1965, to four years and ten months on January 30, 1966. Once again, the desire for lower interest costs seems to have dominated debt management policy.

In summary, we can say that postwar national debt policy seems to have been directed toward securing lower interest costs. Table 6 shows the percentage distribution of national debt by time to maturity since 1946. There have been significant increases in the shorter maturities outstanding.

Relationships Between Federal, State, and Local Debt

Table 7 shows the growth in federal government, state and local government, and private debt from 1950 through 1964. As shown there, state and local government debt exceeded $92 billion on June 30, 1964, and approximated $100 billion in 1966. Of this total, local government debt accounts for about 70 percent. State and local debt has increased nearly four times since 1950. This is in sharp contrast to the approximate 25 percent increase in national debt over the same period. State governments have been increasing their debt more rap-

Table 6

Maturity Distribution of the National Debt, 1946-65
(percentages of total marketable debt)

Fiscal Year Ending June 30	Within 1 Year	1 to 5 Years	5 to 10 Years	10 to 20 Years	20 Years and Over	Average Length (Years-Months)
1946	32.7	13.1	22.0	9.2	23.0	9- 1
1947	30.4	13.0	21.1	11.0	24.6	9- 5
1948	30.4	13.5	20.1	10.2	25.9	9- 2
1949	31.0	21.0	10.8	14.7	22.5	8- 9
1950	27.3	33.0	5.0	18.1	16.6	8- 2
1951	31.8	33.7	6.3	21.7	6.4	6- 7
1952	33.2	33.8	10.0	18.3	4.7	5- 8
1953	44.3	24.5	10.6	19.5	1.1	5- 4
1954	41.5	19.9	18.3	19.0	1.1	5- 6
1955	32.0	25.2	22.1	18.4	2.3	5-10
1956	37.9	22.2	18.7	18.4	2.8	5- 4
1957	46.2	26.1	7.9	17.0	2.8	4- 9
1958	40.7	25.5	12.9	16.6	4.3	5- 3
1959	41.0	32.8	9.6	12.1	4.5	4- 7
1960	38.3	39.6	11.0	6.9	4.2	4- 4
1961	43.3	31.2	14.1	5.5	5.9	4- 6
1962	45.1	29.1	13.3	4.8	7.8	4-11
1963	41.9	28.5	18.4	4.1	7.1	5- 1
1964	39.4	31.7	16.9	4.0	7.9	5- 0
1965	42.0	28.4	18.8	4.0	8.3	5- 4

SOURCE: *Economic Report of the President, 1966*, p. 275.

idly than local governments. The debts of the former have increased nearly five times since 1950 while those of the latter have increased less than four times.

The important distinction between national and state and local government debt lies not in their relative sizes or rates of growth, but in the unique possession of money creation powers held by the national government. State and local debt plays no role in the money creation process, whereas national debt is involved directly. The debt of state and local governments is entirely real; no disguised money creation exists within their debt instruments. The analytical interest in state and local debt is accordingly less than that in national debt because only changes in national debt directly influence the level of economic activity. This is not to deny the importance of state and local government debt. But the problems involved are subsumed within one set of the problems of national government debt.

Table 7

Public and Private Debt, 1950 to 1964
(billions of dollars)

Ending Fiscal Year June 30	Total Debt	Public Debt				Private Debt		
		Total	Federal	State	Local	Total	Corporate	Noncorporate
1950	557.4	281.6	257.4	5.4	18.8	275.8	167.0	108.8
1951	592.6	282.3	255.2	6.4	20.7	310.3	190.6	119.7
1952	625.8	288.7	259.1	7.0	22.6	337.1	201.6	135.5
1953	660.7	298.8	266.1	8.0	24.7	361.9	211.5	150.4
1954	691.0	309.2	271.3	10.2	27.7	381.8	216.3	165.5
1955	758.9	317.6	274.4	11.8	31.4	441.3	251.0	190.3
1956	803.4	320.8	272.8	13.1	34.9	482.6	274.9	207.7
1957	837.9	323.0	270.5	13.7	38.8	514.9	293.4	221.5
1958	877.0	333.5	276.3	15.7	41.5	543.5	305.0	240.3
1959	948.8	347.1	284.7	17.2	45.2	601.7	335.9	265.8
1960	1,001.4	353.4	286.3	18.1	49.0	648.0	361.6	286.4
1961	1,159.3	361.5	289.0	20.0	52.5	697.8	387.5	310.3
1962	1,137.0	379.1	298.2	21.9	59.0	757.9	416.3	341.6
1963	1,221.2	392.6	305.9	23.4	63.3	828.6	449.7	379.0
1964	1,301.8	403.9	311.7	25.0	67.2	897.9	480.3	417.6

SOURCES: 1950-53: *Survey of Current Business*, May, 1957, p. 19; 1954-56: *Ibid.*, May, 1959, p. 12; 1957-59: *Ibid.*, May, 1962, p. 19; 1960-64: *Ibid.*, May, 1965, p. 10.

Relationships Between Public and Private Debt

The growth in private debt has been only slightly less rapid than the growth in state and local government debt, having increased a little over three times between 1950 and 1965. Broken into its major components, corporate debt increased about three times and individual and other noncorporate debt increased about four times. All the relevant figures are shown in Table 7.

Private debt is in the same position as state and local government debt; both types of debt are real because neither state and local governments nor private citizens possess money creation powers. The analytical problems of private and of state and local government debt are equivalent.

The Effect of National Debt on Interest Rates

Since national debt is about 25 percent of all debt in the United States, some brief consideration of the way in which national debt can affect interest rates seems desirable. National debt may affect interest rates in two manners: It can influence the general level of interest rates and it can influence the term structure of interest rates within a given average level.

The general level of interest rates is governed by the supply of and demand for loanable funds. The demand for funds comes from potential borrowers, and the supply comes from potential lenders. The interest rate measures, on one hand, the price that borrowers are willing to pay to secure use of the funds, and on the other, the price that lenders must be paid to induce them to give up current consumption in exchange for future consumption. Thus the intersection of the demand for and the supply of loanable funds, like any demand and supply intersection, determines the price of loanable funds (the interest rate) and the quantity of loanable funds placed on the market.

At first glance, the effect that national debt would have on the level of interest rates seems obvious, but additional considerations confound the situation. An increase in national debt is an increase in the demand for loanable funds (the government increases its demand for funds). If the public expenditure were financed by taxation instead of public borrowing, the demand for loanable funds would fall by the amount of the potential borrowing. Subsequently there would be fewer loanable funds clearing the market and the interest rate would fall. The level of interest rates seems to vary directly with changes in the quantity of national debt. This is probably true, but not nearly in the magnitude suggested by the preceding discussion. Suppose public borrowing is reduced. Taxes must now be raised to accommodate the spending. But the increase in taxes will reduce the supply of loanable funds through a reduction in disposable income. The reduction in public borrowing reduces both the demand for and the supply of loanable funds. National debt influences the level of interest rates, but not in the magnitudes that would be expected from simply looking at the changes in public borrowing.

Additional considerations also suggest that the relative effect of normal national debt transactions on the level of interest rates may be small. Any changes that occur in the national debt are more likely to be in the $3 billion range than in the $300 billion range. Whereas a $300 billion change represents about 25 percent of the $1,200 billion total debt, a $3 billion change represents only about 0.25 percent. Even a $12 billion change in national debt is only 1 percent of total debt, public and private. Thus changes in national debt are unlikely to have a large impact on the level of interest rates because a relatively small part of all borrowing and lending is involved.

National debt also influences the structure of interest rates within the context of an unchanged average interest rate. The structure of interest rates refers to the difference between interest rates of different types of loans. If other relevant factors remain equal, the longer the loan the higher the rate of interest. A higher rate of interest must be paid on a 20-year loan than on a one-year loan; the lender must be compensated an extra amount for the additional liquidity he foregoes in making the longer loan. This is true even if the longer term loan is no riskier than the shorter term loan. The borrower must compensate the lender for the liquidity the latter must forego in making the loan. The longer the term of the loan, the greater the amount of liquidity given up by the lender, and the greater the payment the borrower must make. This simple idea leads to an explanation of the difference in the term structure of interest rates, though additional complicating factors enter to prevent a simple correspondence between the length of the loan and the interest rate. For example, a 20-year high grade corporate bond would probably have a lower interest rate than a one-year bond floated by a speculative firm that intends to search for gold in Virginia. Differences in riskiness can cause some long-term loans to have lower interest rates than other short-term loans, but the explanation of the structure of interest rates says a direct relation will exist between interest rates and time to maturity only for equal-risk loans. When elements of equal riskiness are combined, the explanation seems to fit the facts well. Thus if borrowers are segregated into government, high grade corporate, medium grade corporate, low risk personal (such people usually borrow from commercial banks), and high risk personal (such people usually borrow from finance companies), within each category the longer the loan the higher the interest rate. Yet short-term loans to high risk individuals carry higher rates than long-term loans to high grade corporations. The explanation lies in the variations in levels of riskiness.

In the early 1960s the national government attempted to influence the term structure of interest rates. This policy is commonly called the "twist" because the government attempted to twist the term structure of interest rates by reducing the differential between short-term and long-term interest rates. The government wanted to lower the level of long-term interest rates to stimulate additional investment which would promote more rapid growth. At the same time, faced with balance-of-payments difficulties, it wanted to raise the short-term interest rate to discourage capital outflows to foreign countries. To achieve such a twist, the government must increasingly enter the short-term market and leave the long-term market. The reduced supply of long-term bonds raises their price (which is equivalent to lowering their interest rates). The increased supply of short-term instruments has the opposite effect, short-term interest rates rise. This policy had some effect in the desired direction, although much less than was initially claimed by its advocates.

Since each $12 billion of national debt is only 1 percent of total debt, the government must be prepared to use considerably more than $12 billion of its debt for policy purposes if it is to have a strong effect. Though the government was not prepared to act in this manner, its actions had some effect in narrowing the differential. As an example of the strong effect that national debt operations can have on the structure of interest rates for a short time, there have been instances where the short-term interest rate exceeded the long-term rate. This is due to sudden, heavy Treasury refinancing in the short-term market; the price of securities was driven down, and the interest rate up.

The Role of National Debt in Bank Portfolios

National debt plays an important role in commercial bank portfolios. The major interest in looking at the role of national debt in bank portfolios lies in the role that bank-held debt can serve in expanding or contracting the levels of money and credit. Banks desire their assets to be fully invested, and, at the same time, they want to maintain liquidity reserves for unforeseen contingencies. Government debt suits this purpose admirably. Any excess funds can be invested in government debt. Yet this debt is highly liquid and can be turned readily into money. Banks can buy national debt to put idle reserves in use, and they can sell national debt when they want additional reserves to use as a base to expand loans.

In fact, changes in the ownership of national debt by commercial banks is a good indicator of changes in the level of economic activity; banks try to reduce their holding of national debt in prosperity and increase their holdings as economic activity slackens. Some recent history is illustrative. During the 1954 to 1957 recovery, bank-held debt declined from $63.6 billion to $56.2 billion. Yet the 1957-58 recession saw it shoot back up to $65.3 billion. During the ensuing recovery period, bank-held national debt fell from $65.3 billion in 1958 to $55.3 billion in 1960. Once again, in 1960, banks turned to purchases of national debt when slackened economic activity reduced other uses for their funds; it went from $55.3 billion in 1960 to $65.2 billion in 1962. The subsequent economic expansion saw the bank held debt fall to below $55 billion in 1966. Furthermore, Federal Reserve purchases of national debt between 1962 and 1966 exceeded commercial bank sales. These purchases, of course, allowed for the multiple expansion of the money supply that took place, especially in 1965. The vigorous Federal Reserve purchase of securities in amounts corresponding to the commercial bank sale of government debt stands out in this recent history. It is also notable that the pace of economic activity was more rapid over this period than in any other time in the past ten years. By contrast, during the aborted 1958-60 recovery, the $10 billion commercial bank sale of national debt was covered by only a $1 billion net increase in Federal Reserve holdings of national debt.

THE BURDEN OF PUBLIC DEBT

Introduction

The "burden of public debt" is one of the hardy perennials of controversy among economists. Hopefully, a consensus is emerging on the basic analysis, but earlier agreement has been shattered by the recurrence of rediscovered fallacies. The professional sophistication of scholars has been less reliable than the realism of ordinary men, and much modern analysis translates common notions into the idiom required to refute false theorems.

The analysis in its proper setting is elementary. This makes acceptance difficult for those who by nature seek complexity. The simple questions must be asked before the complex ones can be answered.

Definitions

"Public debt" has been defined. We have not defined "burden." What is meant when we use the term "burden" of public debt, or any debt, since usage extends to private obligations? We proceed by analogy with simpler questions.

The Burden of Taxation. "Burden" is also widely used with reference to taxes. What is meant by "burden of taxes"? When a tax is employed to finance public goods or services, some individuals must give up command over private goods. They surrender purchasing power which is used by government. This sacrifice of private goods, represented in the payments made, is the *burden of taxation.* Who pays the taxes? Who bears the burden? How much does each person pay? If these questions are answered, we have located the opportunity cost of the public goods that are tax-financed.

27

Is it wholly appropriate, however, to speak of the burden of taxes? What we seek is the location of the *opportunity cost* of public goods, and "burden of taxes" is an admittedly clumsy way of speaking here. We may show this by a comparison with the treatment of opportunity cost in private-goods markets. When we try to determine the cost of an apple, we measure this directly through price. The price of the apple represents the value of alternative private goods that could have been purchased in place of the apple. We do not speak about the "burden of price"; but this would be required to make the language comparable. At the most fundamental level of discourse, "price" is a burden in precisely the same sense that a tax is a burden. The coercive nature of most taxes, even in the most democratic of governments, hides the *exchange relationship* that the fiscal process embodies. To an isolated citizen, a tax is a "burden," a load that he must carry, or suffer the penalties. He does not, in his psychology of behavior, consider that his enjoyment of publicly provided goods and services is affected by his own payment or nonpayment of taxes. With "price," things appear, and are, different because of the divisibility of private goods and because of the delineation of property rights. The individual recognizes that failure to pay the price demanded for a unit of private goods will directly result in his own failure to secure that unit for his own enjoyment.

The term "burden" in the discussion of taxes is, therefore, based on common usage that is grounded squarely in the psychology of individual fiscal response. The essential analogy of "taxes" and "prices" must, nonetheless, be emphasized. In a broadly democratic political structure, individuals must, at one stage of decision, consider taxes as the necessary surrender of private goods *in exchange* for public goods. Who pays and in what amounts are vital questions, but payment must be made in exchange *for something,* despite the absence of an individual *quid pro quo.*

The Burden of Debt. Debt issue is an alternative to taxation as a revenue-raising device. What is the opportunity cost of public goods that are financed by debt instead of taxes? Who pays and in what amount? Who bears the "burden of public debt"? Again the terminology is clumsy, but usage dictates language; this need not be damaging so long as the meaning is made clear. In locating opportunity cost under debt financing, a new dimension enters, one that seldom arises with taxes. Who pays? In what amount? *And when?* The *location in time* of the cost or burden becomes important, and it is this new dimension that has created much confusion.

Burden of debt is the *opportunity cost of public goods that are financed through debt issue.* So far, so good; but definitional issues remain. What is meant by opportunity cost? In the standard response this is measured by the value of sacrificed alternatives. With public debt, opportunity cost is the value of private goods that are "given up" *in exchange* for the public goods that debt issue makes possible. But precisely what do we mean by "given up"?

When is cost incurred? This question must be answered even in the case of ordinary market transactions before we go on to the complexities of debt burden. In one sense, all cost is concentrated in the moment of effective decision. Once we have decided to forego the alternatives which we could have purchased instead and decided to purchase a new automobile, we have, forever, given up these foregone alternatives. In a second, and objective, sense, there is no cost incurred until *after* decision when we must pay out funds. Objectively, cost is incurred only at the moment of payment.

In ordinary dealings, these two moments are sufficiently close one to the other, for most purchases, to allow us to forget the distinction. In the treatment of debt burden, when the difference in time is the important new dimension, these two quite distinct opportunity-cost concepts create difficulty. As previously mentioned, the individual bears the subjective cost of the automobile when he decides to make the purchase because he has decided at that time to give up the alternatives that he could purchase. If he pays cash for the automobile, he also bears the objective cost (the observed payout of funds) at the same time. If, however, he buys it on an installment plan, he postpones the objective cost through time. In this case, the objective cost is borne only when the deferred payments are made.

A warning is in order. We should keep in mind that, with every decision, there are two separate opportunity costs, one subjective, the other objective, and that we must always be clear as to which one of the two we refer.

Methodology

What is the purpose of the analysis about debt burden? Why should we worry about who bears the burden and in what time periods? Perhaps truth is attractive for its own sake, but analysis is relatively barren unless correct answers to these questions can lead to better *decisions* than incorrect answers. The appropriate decision-making context must be introduced to make the whole analysis relevant. Who needs to know by whom and when the opportunity costs of debt-financed public goods are paid? What specific choices will be informed?

Public borrowing is an alternative to taxation. When confronted with the necessity of raising revenues to finance a program of public spending, those who make governmental decisions must, somehow, compare the effects of these separate instruments. They must predict what will happen differently if they authorize public borrowing (debt creation) instead of taxation. They need to know the difference in the distribution of the cost of public goods as between these two methods of finance.

Who are the decision makers? In a democratic society, governmental decisions are made by individual citizens, either directly, or indirectly through politically-elected representatives. Both citizens and legislators need to know the fundamentals of public debt. Citizens need to be able to evaluate alternative courses of action. To the extent that legislators are better informed the efficiency of the whole democratic process should be increased.

The Simple Analytics

Consider the choice faced by an individual (as an actual or potential voter in a referendum) between debt issue on the one hand and taxation on the other. To clear away complexities that obscure the basic questions, it will be helpful to make some simplifying assumptions.

Assume that there is widespread, indeed unanimous, agreement that the public-goods project to be financed is highly beneficial to the community. The expected benefits exceed the expected costs; the public commitment of funds is a good investment. Assume that this is true for the community in the aggregate, but, also, that it is true for each individual citizen. This allows purely distributional considerations to be eliminated from the choice problem. Since the real incomes of *all* citizens are increased, questions such as, "Is a $1 net increase in national income desirable if it involves a $2 gain to a Texas cattle raiser and a $1 loss to a West Virginia coal miner?" are excluded because nobody suffers real income reductions. For the individual whose choice we examine, he expects to be made better off by the combined spending-revenue raising operation, regardless of the method of finance.

To simplify his choice even further, assume that he estimates that his own liability will be identical under the two methods of financing.

The present value of the taxes that he must pay *now,* if the tax method is selected, is just equal to the present value of the taxes that he must pay, *in later periods,* in order to service and amortize the debt, should this method be selected.

Confronted with this choice, how will the individual make his decision? What elements will be influential in this choice?

In one sense, the financing alternatives are equivalent, as we have defined them. But an individual need not be indifferent as between the two, unless he can convert one alternative into the other costlessly through the capital market. He may prefer to meet his fiscal obligation through current taxation, or he may prefer to issue debt now and to meet this obligation in later periods. His decision will depend on his time preference. If he desires to *postpone* the objective cost, or payout of funds, he will select, or vote for, debt issue. This is precisely what debt allows him to do, to postpone or put off in time the actual necessity of giving up purchasing power over private goods. This is, at base, the *raison d'être* of debt, whether this be public or private. Debt provides an institutional means of shifting objective opportunity cost forward in time. In our example, the benefits of the public-goods project can be secured now without the necessity that the cost of payment for these goods, the "burden," be incurred simultaneously.

The analysis here is elementary, and it can scarcely be questioned. Indeed it is not questioned by the ordinary citizen who knows that debt, public or private, is a method of postponing cost. The "burden of debt" is located, obviously, in periods subsequent to that of debt issue, subsequent to the period when public outlays are made.

The Ricardian Equivalence Theorem

Using the same example we have introduced here, David Ricardo advanced a theorem about public debt that has been widely discussed for a century and a half. He suggested that there is no difference between public debt and taxation. So long as the present value of the two alternatives remains identical to the individual, the two should be indifferent to the chooser.

This theorem is based on the arithmetic of the discounting process, and it depends for its plausibility upon the assumption of a perfectly working capital market that allows the individual to convert any one time stream of payments into any other without cost. The theorem, even within these limits, tends to obscure important elements of the individual's decision process. Specifically, it fails to distinguish subjective and objective opportunity cost. The fact that the individual's net worth is reduced by the same amount in the two cases (this reduction is offset by the increase in net worth due to the public spending), does not imply subjective equivalence between the two fiscal instruments. With taxes, the payout of funds is current. With debt, this payout is postponed. The individual will prefer one time stream over the other, even with constancy in present value unless he can operate in a perfect capital market.

The Ricardian theorem also tends to obscure, or to neglect, imperfections in the discounting process itself. Even arithmetically, the loan and the tax become equivalent *only* if the individual converts an expected stream of payments into a present value. To the extent that he fails to discount fully the future tax payments that debt issue involves, he will weigh the debt alternative more favorably; his decision will be biased. And, it is the temporal location of objective debt burden that makes this conversion process necessary. If, for some reason, the "burden" of debt should be located in the same period as the burden of equivalent tax, no discounting would be required. In this sense, the whole Ricardian theorem is based on an acceptance of the elementary principle which states that the objective opportunity cost of debt-financed public spending is shifted forward in time.

The Fallacies of Debt Burden

There would be no need for further discussion on "burden of public debt" were it not for the continued refusal of economists to accept the simple principles sketched out above. The denial of these principles is based on a set of intersecting fallacies which must be discussed critically and carefully. The overthrow of these fallacies is important. Despite the emerging agreement among analysts, the fallacies are still to be found in the majority of elementary textbooks in economics. For this reason alone, some attention should be paid to the persuasiveness of the arguments which deny the simple analytics of debt burden.

The several fallacies combine to produce three related conclusions, each one of which is simply wrong. These are:

(1) The primary burden of public debt cannot be shifted forward in time;

(2) Internal public debt is fundamentally different in effect from external public debt;

(3) Internal public debt is not similar to private debt.

Textbooks can be found which make all of these statements. The underlying analysis must, indeed, be convincing. The fallacies are subtle; the reasoning is sophisticated.

The Real-Cost Fallacy. Since the eighteenth century, it has been variously argued that, for the community as a whole, no postponement of cost or burden is possible. In this view, emphasis is placed on the physical usage of economic resources. Public debts have, historically, been associated with war expenditures, and this particular argument has centered on the burden of debt-financed war outlays. The resources that go into armaments, the steel for the guns, so the argument runs, must be drawn directly from the economy during the time period that the guns are made. There can be no putting off in this respect. The real costs of war spending are best represented in the current reductions in private goods, the butter that must be given up in order to produce the guns. This real cost, or burden, of the war spending must be current, whether the actual financing be done through taxation, currency inflation, or through debt creation.

At first glance, this argument is indeed persuasive, and the fallacy that it embodies is not readily discernible. If attention is limited to aggregative effects, nothing seems wrong with the argument. In national accounting terms, public spending is increased implying an increase in public or governmental usage of resources; private spending and private resource usage is decreased. These changes take place regardless of the methods of financing the public expenditures. Debt and taxation appear to be alternative means of allocating the costs of the public goods with no *temporal* difference in the location of these costs as between these two fiscal instruments.

To get at the fallacy here, we must return to the definitional-methodological questions stressed earlier. If public debt, as an institution, does not facilitate a postponement of the opportunity costs of public goods, who pays these costs? If these costs must be incurred in the period when the resources are used, what individuals and groups in the community give up private goods *in exchange* for public goods?

Where do the resources used to make the guns come from? Those persons who purchase the government securities, who buy the bonds, bear the costs of public goods, so this argument goes. But do they? These persons give up command over private goods during the period of debt creation and public outlay. This cannot be questioned. In so doing, these persons bear a cost, shoulder a burden. But to what purpose? What do they secure *in exchange* for this sacrifice of private goods? This question has not been asked by those who advance the real-cost argument.

Once this question is raised, the weakness in the argument is apparent. Those individuals who buy bonds give up private goods *in exchange* for the promises of future income that the bonds embody. They give up nothing at all, in their capacities as bond buyers, in exchange for the public goods that are financed by the debt creation. They do not, in this capacity, participate directly in the fiscal exchange.

The real-cost approach conceals the fact that *public debt involves two separate exchanges.* In the basic fiscal exchange, individuals, in their capacities as voters-taxpayers-beneficiaries, secure the benefits of public spending in exchange for their own promises to pay interest and principal on bonds in future periods. In the facilitating financial exchange, individuals, in their capacities as bond buyers, secure these promises of future income in exchange for their own sacrifice of purchasing power in the current period. The bond buyers give up current private goods in order to secure future income, not in order to secure public goods. The voters-taxpayers give up no current private goods; they secure the benefits of the public goods by promising to give up private goods in future periods. *Future* taxpayers pay for the goods when they make their payments to the bondholders.

This dual exchange is clearly revealed when the nature of bond purchase is noted. Those who buy instruments suffer no net reduction in private wealth in the process. No one else gives up purchasing power in the period of actual public outlay. From this it would seem to follow that, if there are no costs shifted forward, the spending is financed without sacrifice. In such reasoning, why should taxes ever be levied? Tax financing clearly imposes current real costs; some individuals will find their private wealth reduced. The public spending may be highly beneficial in each case; but with tax financing this is netted against some reduction in private income and wealth. With debt financing, if the real-cost argument holds, there need be no netting out; there is no offsetting reduction in private income and wealth to put against the benefits of public spending. National accounting should also pay attention to those effects on individual balance sheets. When this is done, the elementary principles of public debt become evident and the real-cost fallacy is not likely to appear.

The Internal Accounting Fallacy. A closely related, but different, argument lends support to the three wrong conclusions about the burden of public debt. The central fallacy here is one of simple accounting.

In the analysis of debt burden above, care was taken not to specify who purchases the bonds when debt is issued. For this initial summary of elementary principles, it makes no difference whether the persons who buy the bonds are citizens or foreigners. At this level of discussion, the distinction between internal (domestic) public debt and external (foreign) public debt is almost wholly irrelevant. In either case, individuals, in their capacities as voters-taxpayers-beneficiaries, borrow funds from other individuals who indicate a willingness to lend. The fact that the lenders may, in some situations, be members of the same political group as the borrowers is not germaine to the analysis. Even if the two groups should be identical, individuals would be acting in two separate capacities.

In sharp contrast with the simple analysis that we presented, the arguments that reach the three wrong conclusions about debt burden depend critically on the distinction between internally-held and externally-held public debt. On the purchase and retention of public debt by foreigners, on external debt, there has been relatively little disagreement. Most scholars, along with ordinary citizens, have accepted the elementary principles. External debt allows a postponement of the opportunity cost of the public goods that are financed, and this cost is measured by the interest and amortization charges that must be paid in time periods after issue. From this it also follows that external public debt is acknowledged to be like private debt, at least in its essential effects.

The controversy has raged only about the burden of *internal* public debt. It is argued that this debt involves no postponement of burden, that it is different from both external debt and private debt in essential respects.

Why should the location of debt burden in time depend so critically on just who happens to buy the bonds? Why should external debt differ so fundamentally from an internal debt? Does it really matter so much that a London bank or a German businessman buys a United States bond? How does this choice affect the economic position of an American taxpayer?

There is a confusion in the simple accounting here, and an example will be helpful in clarification.

Consider a small community with only two persons, Mr. A and Mr. B, who are assumed to be identical in most respects. Before the issue of public debt, the partial balance sheets of the two citizens are as follows:

BEFORE PUBLIC DEBT AND BEFORE PUBLIC SPENDING

Mr. A		Mr. B	
Cash $100		Cash $100	
	Net Worth $100		Net Worth $100

We now assume that the community (AB) decides to finance a public-goods project by debt issue. For purposes of keeping our illustration simple, let us assume that the project will yield benefits just equal to its cost of $100. Assume further that the benefits are to be shared equally by A and B.

Now consider an issue of internal public debt. Let us suppose that Mr. A buys the single bond of $100. How will the two balance sheets look immediately after the project is constructed?

AFTER INTERNAL PUBLIC DEBT AND AFTER PUBLIC SPENDING

Mr. A		Mr. B	
Cash 0		Cash $100	
Bond $100			
Benefit	Future Tax	Benefit	Future Tax
Value	(Present	Value	(Present
Project $ 50	Value) $ 50	Project $ 50	Value) $ 50
	Net Worth $100		Net Worth $100

Note that there has been no change in the net worth of either of the two persons as a result of the combined public-spending, debt-issue operation. This is guaranteed by the assumption that the project is just worth its cost. Net worth of both persons would, of course, have been increased if the project is more than marginally beneficial, and vice versa.

We want to compare this result with that which is produced when the bond is sold to foreigners. Consider the partial balance sheets of A and B after this operation and with the same public project.

AFTER EXTERNAL PUBLIC DEBT AND AFTER PUBLIC SPENDING

Mr. A		Mr. B	
Cash $100 Benefit Value Project $ 50	Future Tax (Present Value) $50 Net Worth $100	Cash $100 Benefit Value Project $ 50	Future Tax (Present Value) $ 50 Net Worth $100

The conclusion to be drawn from these elementary T-accounts is evident. There is no difference in the net worth of the two persons as between internal and external public debt.

Why has this extremely simple accounting identity been implicitly denied by those who make so much of the difference between these two forms of public debt? The real-cost fallacy, already discussed, is partially responsible. When bonds are sold externally, resources for public-goods production are actually drawn from outside the economic limits of the political community. There is a physically-observed resource flow across political boundaries. In the initial period, during which both the bonds are sold and the public-goods project is constructed, no resources from inside the economy, no domestic resources, are diverted from private to public uses. For the observer who looks superficially at such physical resource flows, and at these only, no real cost seems to be incurred in this initial period. No member of the community is observed to be giving up or sacrificing current command over private goods and services. The fact that, in balance-sheet terms, precisely the same thing happens with external and with internal debt has been almost wholly overlooked.

This oversight has been reinforced by the tendency of scholars to ask the wrong questions about debt burden. There has been an undue concentration on defining the *burden of carrying an existing debt,* as opposed to the relevant question concerning the burden of a potential debt about to be created. If a public debt exists, whether this be internally or externally held, there is, of course, a burden. But the location of this burden or cost is relevant only if and when a decision is to be made about the issue of new debt or the retirement of old debt.

If attention is exclusively concentrated on defining the burden of an existing public debt, internal and external debt appear to exert different effects, and the internal acounting fallacy is more subtle. In order to service and to amortize external debt, resources must be transferred out of the boundaries of the political unit; payments must be made to foreign holders of the bonds. This is not necessary when bonds are held by local citizenship interest and amortization payments are made within the economy. From this rather obvious difference it would seem to follow that, *other things equal,* an externally-held debt is more "burdensome" than an internally-held debt of like amount.

This seemingly straightforward analysis disregards the fact that *other things cannot be equal* in this situation. To see this clearly, it is necessary to return to the period when the existing debt was issued and to trace out the effects on individual balance sheets, as we have done with the simple T-accounts above. When external debt is issued, when bonds are sold to foreigners, resources are drawn from outside the economy. These *additional* resources replace domestic resources that would otherwise be used for public-goods production. There are more resources that remain invested in the domestic economy, and these resources yield a return that is sufficient to service fully the external debt, provided only that the loan was made on competitive terms. Regardless of the productivity of the public spending that is financed by the debt, the assets of individual citizens that are held in the form of claims *other than public debt instruments* must be higher, in a one-to-one correspondence, than these claims would be under an internal debt issue of the same quantity. These assets will yield a normal return which will provide resources sufficient to pay interest charges on externally-held debt. Once this fact is recognized, it cannot be argued that the external debt is more "burdensome."

The Transfer-Payment Fallacy. "We owe it to ourselves." This is a familiar refrain in the argument of those who deny that internal public debt shifts cost forward in time and who claim that this debt is different in kind from both external public debt and private debt. This brings to attention another strand of the interrelated argument that is more modern than those previously discussed. The post-Keynesian emphasis on national accounting is partially responsible for the reigning intellectual confusion. In such accounting, balance sheets and income statements are drawn, not for separate individuals, but for aggregates, with more or less arbitrary limits at politically-determined boundaries. Debits and credits in individual accounts are often mutually cancelling and, to this extent, they may not affect national totals.

This has given credence to the false argument about the burden of internal debt. If those who hold public debt instruments, the government securities, live within the national economy, the interest payments made to them out of taxes collected within the economy are treated as transfer payments, not as income. No resources are used up in making these transfers; the interest payments are not made in exchange for current goods and services.

The fallacy here lies in the implication that the treatment of particular sorts of payments in the conventions of national accounting can, in some manner, modify the location of opportunity cost of public goods. At best, these conventions are arbitrary and many of them are subject to serious criticism. If the government (individuals in their collectively-organized capacities) chooses not to default on its debt obligation, the transfer-payment characteristic of service charges on internally-held debt does not modify, in the slightest, the economic circumstances of the individual who is a member of the community.

Interest payments on private debts held internally are included in national income (except for inter-household payments). But these are transfers in precisely the same sense as are interest payments on public debt. In both cases, interest payments represent transfers of income from individuals, in their capacities as borrowers-debtors, to individuals, in their capacities as lenders-creditors. In both cases, these payments are contractual. The mere fact that, for convenience in national accounting, only one of these two types of payment is treated explicitly as a transfer is wholly irrelevant to the analysis of debt burden.

Principles of Debt Burden Summarized

The circuitous, and sometimes devious, argument through which the simple principles of public debt have been denied is grounded on several related fallacies in logical reasoning. The dispelling of these fallacies serves to establish more firmly the validity of the common-sense principles. These may be summarized in a form that reverses each one of the erroneous conclusions noted earlier.

Contrary to much modern argument, we conclude:

(1) Public debt, as a financing institution, allows individual members of a political community to postpone the objective opportunity costs of public goods. The primary burden of public debt is shifted forward in time.

(2) There is no essential difference between internal public debt and external public debt.

(3) Public debt and private debt are similar in the most basic respects. In the former, individuals borrow funds in their capacities as citizens; in the latter, they borrow funds in their capacities as private economic units.

Secondary Burdens and Benefits of Publc Debt

In the primary fiscal exchange, the "burden of public debt" offsets the benefits received from the public goods that are debt financed. Debt issue, like most fiscal actions, also generates indirect and secondary effects. Our treatment to this point has left these out of account. We should expect these indirect effects to involve both costs and benefits. Debt issue, quite apart from the primary effects already discussed, generates indirect burdens on some members of the community which are balanced against indirect and secondary benefits conferred on other members.

Interest Rates, Borrowers, and Lenders. When the government sells securities, bond prices fall and interest rates rise. As compared with tax financing for the same public expenditure, loan financing implies relatively higher interest rates. This indirectly affects the economic positions of individuals in several ways. An increase in interest rates decreases the capitalized values of all fixed-yield assets and claims; creditors holding such claims find their net wealth decreased. Offsetting this, debtors who owe fixed charges find their capitalized liabilities decreased, for the same reasons.

Similar offsetting effects involve prospective lenders and prospective borrowers. With debt financing, the individual who accumulates funds for lending is benefited by the increase in rates; the individual who seeks to accelerate his time stream of outlay through borrowing privately is harmed.

The Accumulation of Capital. Public debt creation, as compared to tax-financing of the same public expenditure, also modifies the rate at which capital formation in the economy takes place. Funds for the purchase of government securities are more likely to be drawn from investment in the private economy than are funds for the payment of taxes. Debt financing involves a relatively greater reduction in private investment spending and a relatively smaller reduction in current consumption spending than does tax financing. As a result, the rate of economic growth is likely to be somewhat lower under debt financing.

This effect, which is indirect, should not be confused with the forward shifting of the primary burden or cost of public goods already discussed. This primary shifting forward occurs regardless of the source of the funds used to purchase government securities. The capital-formation effect involves an additional, and secondary, reduction in income in periods subsequent to debt issue. In one sense, this may also be called a "burden" that is shifted in time. Individuals who live in post-debt periods will suffer some relative reduction in income flows.

Offsetting this "burden," however, there is an indirect and secondary benefit conferred by debt issue on those individuals who live and earn incomes during the initial period of debt-issue and public spending. Relative to the tax financing alternative, they are allowed to maintain a higher level of current consumption. These individuals benefit at the expense of individuals who live in later periods.

THE CREATION AND RETIREMENT
OF PUBLIC DEBT

Introduction

We can now examine public policy on public debt. Under what conditions is it appropriate for governments, national and state-local, to finance expenditures by borrowing? When, if ever, should public debt be retired?

Before we can even get at these questions, the purpose of the whole fiscal operation must be specified. Debt issue is one means of financing public spending, but this spending may be aimed at providing public goods or at stimulating total demand in the economy. It will be necessary to distinguish between the "fiscal policy" or "macroeconomic" objectives of debt issue or retirement and the "public goods" or "cost distribution" objectives of the same fiscal operations.

Public Debt as an Instrument of Macroeconomic Policy

We shall first discuss the creation and retirement of public debt under the assumption that the objectives for policy are limited to effects on the overall level of demand in the economy. The implied norms toward public-debt creation and retirement will vary with the macroeconomic setting. It is necessary to look at these operations under conditions first of deficient total demand and, secondly, under conditions of excessive total demand.

1(a). *Public Debt Creation in Recession.* If budgetary deficits are created for the express purpose of stimulating total demand in the economy, public debt should *never* be used as the means of financing

43

44

these deficits, so long as the government possesses money-creating power. This rule is applicable to national governments, which do possess such money-creating powers. If it is desirable to add to total demand in the economy through deficit spending, the financing of deficits should not be done in such a way as to offset, in whole or in part, the effects of the accelerated rate of public spending relative to taxation. Funds should not be withdrawn from private uses when they can be created costlessly by the utilization of money-creating power. Public debt issue in such circumstances is clumsy and inefficient, and it imposes wholly unnecessary costs on future taxpayers through the interest charges.

The fiscal policy norm here is straightforward. Yet it is in precisely this setting that many scholars advocate public debt issue. The blatant disregard for elementary logic that this advocacy suggests is explained by the widespread confusion between genuine debt issue and money creation. Optimally, deficits should be financed with new money in such situations. No funds are withdrawn from private uses in this operation, and no costs are shifted forward in time. But modern methods of money creation involve so-called "borrowing" from central banks, from the Federal Reserve banks in this country. Semantic confusion has distorted economics, and there has been a continuing failure to make the vital distinction between "public debt," as a mere pseudonym for "disguised money creation," and "public debt," the real McCoy, interest-bearing obligations sold to the non-bank public. Unfortunately, this particular confusion seems to be permanently implanted in the language of budgetary and fiscal policy. Little, if any progress, has been made in clarification since Henry Simons of the University of Chicago eloquently called attention to the confusion more than two decades past.

If governments do not possess money-creating powers (for example, state-local government) or if, from some political-institutional reason, resort to this alternative is ruled out, deficit financing by debt issue may be warranted during periods of deficient demand. In this latter case, debt issue remains a second-best means of financing; money creation remains the efficient financing instrument. In issuing debt, it must be recognized that funds are withdrawn from private uses and that this offsets, to some extent, the initially-desired effects of deficit spending. The offsets under debt financing will be less than those that might be expected under tax financing, which would be, in this case, the only available alternative.

1(b). *Public Debt Retirement in Recession.* If public debt is to be paid off, retired, funds must come either from taxation or from money creation. In periods when total demand in the economy is deficient, the combined levy of taxes and debt repayment will, on balance, make matters worse rather than better. The expansionary effects of the retirement of debt will be more than offset by the restrictive effect of collecting the taxes.

The retirement of debt from money creation, by contrast, will be clearly expansionary. Liquidity in the economy will be increased by the substitution of money for securities, and there will be no restrictive offsets in the financing side. In addition, new funds will be made available for private investments, with beneficial results for the long-term rate of economic growth.

This policy combination is feasible if budgetary deficits are not created, if reliance is placed on "monetary" rather than "fiscal" policy in accomplishing macroeconomic objectives. The monetary authority, considered as a part of government, effectively carries out this policy when it purchases government securities in the open market. Politically, it can be predicted that fiscal policy instruments will normally be introduced in periods when demand is deficient. The "easy-money" alternative, which involves effective retirement of public debt, seems unlikely to be politically acceptable.

2(a). *Public Debt Creation in Inflation.* Precisely the opposing policy mix is suggested when demand is excessive, when inflation threatens. If fiscal policy instruments are not used, if budgets remain neutral, a "hard money" policy, represented by the sale of government securities in the open market by the monetary authority can eliminate the inflationary pressures. This policy amounts, in effect, to public debt issue, although it is not often explicitly recognized as such. But the net result is an increase in the holdings of government obligations by the public and a decrease in the holdings by the central bank, which for purposes of this discussion should be considered as a part of government itself. The fact that the nominally-measured totals for national debt include those securities held in Federal Reserve bank portfolios should not obscure the simple economics of the operation.

By contrast with the "easy money" policy during recession, this debt-issue operation during inflation is likely to be politically much more predictable than fiscal-policy alternatives. Budget surpluses are not likely to be created deliberately so long as the less direct monetary policy alternative can be utilized.

2(b). *Public Debt Retirement in Inflation.* Central banks should not purchase government securities from the public when inflationary pressures are present in the economy. "Monetary policy" norms suggest the opposing course of action. If fiscal policy should be employed as the restrictive instrument, despite the political odds against this possibility, taxes will produce revenues in excess of current spending rates; budget surpluses will be created. In such situations, strong pressures will emerge to retire outstanding issues of public debt from such surplus revenues. If this is done, however, some of the restrictive effects of the surplus creation will be offset through the return of the funds back to the economy through debt retirement. This half of the operation, in and of itself, is expansionary, and is not desirable during inflation. Budgetary surpluses should be used to build up Treasury cash balances or to retire "fake debt" held in the central bank, the latter being the modern institutional means of destroying money.[1]

Public Debt and Built-In Fiscal Flexibility. Deliberate fiscal policy action designed to create budgetary deficits in periods of deficient aggregate demand and to create budgetary surpluses in periods of excessive demand can be described more easily than it can be accomplished. The recognition of the difficulties of short-run adjustments in fiscal policy has provided the basis for a long-range policy that contains automatic or built-in adjustments as the situation in the economy changes. Budgetary policy under this alternative is aimed at balancing expected tax revenues against public spending when the economy is generating "full-employment GNP." If the tax and the expenditure structures contain built-in and disproportionate reactions to national income change, this policy will insure that deficits are automatically created during periods of deficient demand and that surpluses are created when demand is excessive.

For the same reasons discussed above, it is not desirable that deficits created under this rule of policy be financed with the issue of public debt. This would withdraw funds from the private economy, which would, in turn, offset to an extent the purpose of the automatic deficit creation. Similarly, budget surpluses that emerge under the operation of this rule should not be used to retire outstanding national debt. This would offset the restrictive effect of the surplus.

---

[1] The collection of taxes, combined with an employment of these revenues to retire public debt held by the Federal Reserve Banks, reduces commercial bank reserves directly. This reduction makes some overall contraction in bank loans outstanding necessary, provided, of course, that banks do not have excess reserves. The latter is unlikely during inflation.

If we disregard here all of the problems that arise in defining satisfactorily just what "full-employment GNP" is and assume that the rule is operative, the deficits should be financed by money creation and the budgetary surpluses should be used to destroy money.

Public Debt and Incorrectly Unbalanced Budgets. Macroeconomic policy instruments are clumsy at best, and they may well be applied incorrectly, both in direction and in magnitude. Predictions of a recession may be widespread, but later evidence may reveal that the real danger was inflation. Alternatively, inflationary pressures may appear persistent, when in fact recession is just around the corner. Given the high degree of uncertainty involved in predicting the economic weather at any time, there is a relatively high probability that fiscal policy action may be incorrectly taken by the time the effects of the action take hold.

In such circumstances, the offsetting effects of public debt creation and repayment can be helpful. Suppose, for example, that a deficit is proposed and that these plans are committed for a fiscal year. During the period, however, let us suppose that excessive rather than deficient demand becomes the problem. It may not be at all feasible to reverse the deficit-spending policy in mid-year, but the manner of financing the deficit may be employed in a corrective way. In this situation, an attempt should be made to finance the deficit by the issue of public debt, not by money issue.

Similar conclusions apply, in reverse, when surpluses are incorrectly projected. Tax reductions and/or spending rates cannot be changed precipitously, for political-institutional reasons. The emerging, and unwanted, surpluses can be used to repay debt held by the public. This action will return to the private spending stream some of the tax revenues that, at this stage, seem to be untimely withdrawals.

Public Debt and the Cost of Public Goods

We have discussed public policy toward public debt on the assumption that macroeconomic objectives are dominant. We have not introduced the classical problem of debt policy. Leaving aside macroeconomics, when should governments borrow? When should debt be repaid?

Any fiscal action will, of course, exert macroeconomic effects, but we shall now assume that these are counterbalanced, if desired, in some satisfactory manner. Our concern here is with the appropriateness or inappropriateness of debt issue and debt retirement as means of distributing the cost of public goods over time.

Consider an example of historical relevance. Before the Interstate Highway Act of 1956, there was considerable discussion as to whether the national government should or should not authorize the issue of special bonds to finance the initial investment in the interstate highway system. This discussion was largely divorced from the effects that such bond financing might have on the macroeconomic variable in the economy. The debate centered on the classical problem: Was it desirable to issue debt to finance public spending on highways? Similar problems may be raised in connection with currently advanced proposals for major federal outlays for urban redevelopment, for water pollution, or for transportation systems. Can an argument be made out to finance these outlays by public debt rather than by taxation?

The classical problem also arises with respect to the retirement of outstanding debt. Apart from the effects of such a policy on the economy in the aggregate, can an argument be advanced for levying current taxes sufficient to repay public debt in some systematic fashion?

Public Borrowing, Public Consumption, and Public Investment. When should taxes be replaced by borrowing? When should the objective cost of public goods be postponed? These are normative questions, and different persons may answer them differently. No hard and fast rules that can be laid down are likely to command universal assent.

Consider, first, the question of financing public spending that supplies goods for current consumption. An example might be the salaries of policemen. Should this type of public spending be financed by debt? Principles of orthodox or "sound" finance suggest that taxation should finance all such public activities. But these principles have little direct economic content, and we need to seek their justification in historical experience rather than logic.

The analogy with private borrowing for consumption purposes seems close. As a rule of prudence, individuals should, perhaps, be discouraged from going into debt for consumption spending. But it is acknowledged that such loans may be desirable in certain circumstances. So long as due attention is paid to the effects of borrowing on future credit worthiness and to the costs involved in carrying deadweight debt, individuals may rationally borrow to support consumption outlays.

There seems little, if any, difference between norms for individual behavior in the private economy and those for behavior in the public economy. Orthodox rules against debt financing of current public consumption may well be supported through reference to the experience of governments, but these rules are not derivable from a rational decision calculus.

The conventions limit government borrowing to (1) extraordinary or emergency spending, and (2) spending for projects that are in the nature of public investments. It will be helpful to discuss these two categories separately.

Wars or defense emergencies require outlays that are extraordinarily high and which are not expected to recur. Full tax financing of expenditures of this type might dictate major shifts in rate structures and in the institutions of taxation. Adverse influences on incentives may arise if this is attempted. So long as spending rates are predicted to fall back to near-normal trend levels after the emergency and so long as the emergency is expected to be reasonably short-lived, debt financing allows for greater stability in the tax structure over time. As we know, an overwhelmingly large share of existing public debts has been created in such situations. For example, during World War II in the United States, full tax financing seemed clearly infeasible. Much of the war outlay was financed by money creation, in part disguised as debt. Once the economy reached full-employment levels of production, this latter means of financing itself became a form of indirect taxation through inflation. But, over and above tax financing, a major share of the war financing was through public debt issue; and there seems to have been widespread agreement that resort to debt issue in these circumstances was fully justified.

The orthodoxy also supports public resort to loans when the spending is for long-term projects that are expected to yield benefits over a whole series of time periods. There are two separate arguments in defense of borrowing to finance public investment projects. The first is the same as that discussed above; the initial outlay is likely to be higher than that incurred in subsequent periods. The bunching of public expenditure in time need not imply a corresponding bunching of cost. Debt issue provides a means of smoothing out the time stream of cost, and the analogy is often drawn to borrowing by business firms to finance their own capital outlays.

A second argument is based on equity considerations. If members of the community in future time periods are to secure the benefits of the public investment (say, a highway system), why should they not pay a share in the cost? Why should individuals bear the full cost during the initial period when the investment takes place, which would tend to be the result under full tax financing?

The proposal for the introduction of *capital budgeting,* as an institutional reform, is based to some extent on an acceptance of these orthodox conventions concerning public borrowing. This scheme allows the separation of public investment outlay from public consumption outlay, and, by inference, different fiscal rules can be applied to the different budgetary components. Capital budgeting has never secured widespread support at the national level in the United States, and even the nominal enthusiasm expressed for the proposal in the early 1960s soon dissipated. Several European countries make a distinction between capital items and current consumption items in their budgets, but the net effects of this purely institutional difference on budgetary policy are not readily discernible. The problem concerns just what items are to be included in capital budget. The differences between public investment and public consumption items can be all too easily exaggerated by reasoning from simple abstract models.

A final argument that lends independent support to the orthodox conventions, but which has not itself been a part of the tradition, stems from a consideration of the politics of the budgetary process in democratic societies. Unless debt financing is authorized for long-term projects, these will tend to be neglected in budget making. Current taxpayers, through their elected representatives, are not likely to support public spending projects that promise benefits only or even predominantly in future periods of time. With a requirement of full tax financing of all projects, budgets will tend to be biased against long-term investment projects. Debt financing tends to eliminate this sort of distortion in political choice. For quite similar reasons, open resort to debt financing for short-term or consumption projects will produce bias toward excessive public spending. The realities of democratic procedures suggest that there is much to be said for the old-fashioned "principles of sound finance."

Systematic Retirement of Public Debt. Following World War I, the national debt of the United States was substantially reduced because of an avowed policy of repayment, often associated with Mellon's tenure as Secretary of the Treasury. Following World War II, no such debt retirement policy was introduced, and the national debt has been allowed to increase gradually and almost continuously over the ensuing years. This dramatic difference in policy between these two postwar periods does not necessarily suggest that one policy was correct and the other wrong. The difference may suggest, instead, that no fully acceptable rules on debt retirement may be laid down; the policy to be followed may depend on the preferences of the decision makers.

Should a long-range policy of systematic debt repayment be introduced, what would be its effects, disregarding the macro-economic aspects already discussed? The collection of taxes in excess of current budgetary outlays and the use of surplus revenues to pay off maturing issues of debt will reduce, permanently, the costs imposed on future taxpayers. Debt retirement in the late 1960s, for example, would reduce the taxes on the individuals living during the 1970s by the amount required to finance the interest charges. The recognition of this elementary fact suggests the absence of any clearly defined policy norm. Most of the existing national debt came into being during the financing of World War II. Why should tax-payers of the late 1960s be forced to do more than to pay service charges on the existing debt? Why should this particular group of taxpayers place on themselves a cost for which they are not more responsible than will be the members of the taxpaying group in the 1970s?

A policy of systematic debt retirement would have to be based on a clearly-expressed preference to relieve future taxpayers of the residual opportunity costs of financing World War II. This preference may, of course, be legitimately held by some members of the community, but it has no intrinsic advantage over the opposing preference. Again recognizing political realities, debt-retirement policies similar to those adopted in the 1920s seem out of the question in the last third of the century.

With much state-local debt, and with particular types of national debt, an argument for systematic repayment can be made more firmly. This debt may not be deadweight in the same sense as debt created to finance past wars. If debt was issued to finance specific public investment projects, a strong case can be advanced for insuring amortization over the period when benefits from the investment are received. This argument receives support from the analogy with business finance and from ordinary considerations of equity.

National Debt Repayment Through Monetization. National debt, if it is to be repaid, must absorb funds from either tax collections or the creation of new money. A policy of systematic repayment from tax sources does not seem possible in the foreseeable future. On the other hand, some considerable repayment of debt through monetization seems both plausible and practicable. When we examined debt retirement during recessions above, monetization was briefly discussed as one element in a contracyclical macroeconomic policy. A more significant prospect for monetization lies in the structural arrangements that may be made for long-range growth in the national monetary stock.

In a growing national economy, new monetary resources must be made available continuously if product price levels are not to fall. One means of adding to the monetary stock is through a deliberate policy of debt monetization. If the budget is kept in rough balance over the cycle, the monetary authority can simply create new money and inject this into the economy by the purchase of debt instruments in the open market. This can be a continuous process, interrupted only by short-range adjustment to macroeconomic objectives. Over time, a substantial reduction in the debt held outside the central bank may be accomplished through this policy.

The effects of this debt monetization policy will be similar to those that would result from debt retirement from tax collections. The cost on future taxpayers will be eliminated to the extent that debt-service charges are removed. The monetization prospect is more practicable, however, because this policy combination does not seem to impose burdens on current taxpayers. In a relative or differential sense, it does impose such burdens. This is because, in the absence of debt monetization, the alternative policy for injecting new money is the creation of continuous budgetary deficits with these being financed by money issue. In this case, either taxes could be reduced or public spending rates expanded, by comparison with the situation under the policy of systematic debt monetization.

National Debt Amortization Through Inflation. There is still another means through which the burden of existing public debt can be reduced in a real sense. If the fiscal-monetary policy is such as to generate serious and continuous inflation in the price level, the real value of the fixed service charges on public debt is continuously eroded. In effect, public debt is retired by taxes imposed on the holders of the debt instruments themselves. Their contractual claim to interest charges, fixed in monetary units, is progressively reduced in real value. In partial remedy for this some countries have introduced fixed purchasing power bonds, which guarantee interest payments in units of fixed purchasing power. To the extent that such bonds are issued, inflation cannot, of course, become a means of retiring public debt.

Real levels of national debt tend to be notoriously low in countries with a long history of inflation because such confiscation of the values of fixed claims has made lenders reluctant to purchase government bonds. By contrast, real levels of debt tend to be relatively high in those countries which have the best records of long-range monetary stability. Inflationary retirement of public debt has much in common with default; governments that resort to this alternative effectively shut off debt financing as a prospective source of funds. In countries with inflationary histories, taxation and currency creation are the only practicable alternatives for financing public spending.

NATIONAL DEBT IN THE 1970s

Predictions

There will be no return to the "sound finance" of the 1920s. A deliberate policy of systematic repayment of national debt from tax-financed budgetary surpluses seems beyond the realm of current political plausibility.

One relatively secure prediction can be made. At the national government level, the United States will probably continue to experience budget deficits more or less continuously, as it has over the postwar years. This result is insured and reinforced by the Keynesian domination of macroeconomic policy discussion. The continued gradual erosion of balanced-budget norms can also be anticipated.

As noted earlier, however, budgetary deficits need not imply debt issue. The prediction of deficits suggests a growth in national debt only to the extent that money creation is not utilized. This prompts a second relatively secure prediction. The confusion in discussion between public debt and money will persist, although hopefully this monograph may contribute to clarification. To the extent that the confusion persists, deficits will probably be financed partially by money creation, disguised and discussed as public debt, and partially by genuine debt. Some growth in national debt can be anticipated. This may be offset, again in part, by monetization. As monetary needs of the economy expand, the Federal Reserve banks may gradually acquire a larger share of national debt outstanding. This, in effect, reduces the real magnitude of national debt, regardless of the language used. It seems unlikely, however, that an explicit policy of debt monetization will be adopted.

55

These considerations allow us to predict a gradual increase in the nominal size of the national debt accompanied by a somewhat lower, but still continuous, increase in the size of the real obligation that the debt represents. This process can continue for several decades, barring some new emergency, without the national debt becoming unduly "burdensome," and without the national government facing "bankruptcy." The balanced-budget norm has been eroded, but modern rules of fiscal prudence tend to limit the national debt in its relation to gross national product. It seems highly unlikely that, during the 1970s, the size of the official national debt will be allowed to exceed, say, 50 percent of GNP. This places the popular clamor about national debt in perspective. It is improper, in the late 1960s, to worry unduly about the existing national debt, in terms either of its principal sum or its annual interest charges. This word of caution against excessive worry can be expressed, however, without denying that a burden does, in fact, exist.

The Debt Limit

Concern about the continuous growth in the official national debt finds its political expression in the periodic congressional debates over raising the authorized debt limit. In May, 1966, the House Ways and Means Committee approved a proposal to increase this limit to $330 billion. The legal status of the debt limit is not clear, since an excess of appropriations over revenue collections might require debt creation in conflict with debt-limit legislation. The periodic debates serve primarily a publicizing function; they draw attention to the national debt, despite the weaknesses in the orthodox measures.

This function of the legal debt limit may be a useful one, but there may also be effects which are adverse and clearly undesirable. In order to avoid the necessity to ask for continual shifts upward in the legal limits, governmental agencies and officials attempt to finance various federal expenditures through ways that do not fall within the nominally measured totals for national debt. Various schemes for so-called "back-door financing" are to be found, and these can only make for fiscal irresponsibility.

Implicit National Debt

The general problem involved in concealing genuine debt obligations from the public and its elected representatives is much more serious than those involving the size and rate of increase in the official national debt. Insofar as the national government obligates itself to transfer income to specific persons in future periods of time, national debt is created, whether or not this be called debt in the technical sense. Such obligations may not represent orthodox contractual returns for the transfer of borrowed funds. They may, instead, represent the promised return for current "insurance" payments. Specifically, we refer here to the implicit national debt that the Old-Age and Survivors' Trust Fund Account (the Social Security Account) embodies. Contributors to this fund account pay current taxes in the expectation that they will, upon retirement, receive specific monthly payments. These promises to pay are debt obligations no less than those represented in government bonds, and they should be treated as such. These obligations may be offset by accumulated fund balances and by present value of current tax liabilities extended into the future. But the actuarial integrity of the Social Security Account is widely known to have been lost long since. On balance, this account represents, in 1966, something more than $400 billion of net debt, a sum larger than the total official national debt.[1] By this net debt, we refer to the fact that, in 1966, the present value of future pension rights in the system, even at current benefit rates, exceeds the present value of future tax collections, at current rates, plus accumulated reserves, by more than $400 billion. Unless the whole system is to default on these obligations, future-period taxpayers will be subjected to a cost of $400 billion over and beyond the taxes that they expect to pay at current rates. This is clearly equivalent, in effect, to an outstanding national debt of like amount. We suggest that this social security debt be made explicit, and that each increase in such debt, through an increase in promised benefit payments not matched by increases in tax rates, also be fully recognized. This monograph is not, obviously, the appropriate place for extended discussion of the many problems of the Social Security Account. The relation to the official national debt is, however, clear. It would indeed be folly if undue or unwarranted attention placed on official national debt totals should blind us to the more serious issues involved in the various "unofficial" debt obligations, by far the most important of which is the Social Security Account.[2]

---

[1] Prior to the 1965 amendments this value was estimated in the range of $321 billion. See, Robert J. Myers, *Long-Range Cost Estimates for Old-Age, Survivors, and Disability Insurance Under the 1956 Amendments* (U.S. Department of Health, Education, and Welfare, Actuarial Study No. 48), p. 20. The 1965 amendments seem surely to have increased this to the estimated range of $400 billion and beyond.

[2] The proposal suggested here is explicitly advanced in James M. Buchanan and Colin Campbell, "Must Social Security Be Compulsory?", *Wall Street Journal* (forthcoming).

The Scholar and Public Policy

Much of our discussion of debt burden involved the refutation of arguments advanced by those who have denied the simple principles. This provokes a question about the controversy itself. Why have competent professional scholars failed to accept the results of what is surely an elementary analytical exercise? There is no problem of theoretical complexity; no mathematical or statistical sophistication is demanded.

The answer seems all too clear. Many modern scholars have sensed what they have felt to be a fundamental conflict between macroeconomic policy prescriptions and the implications of public-debt analysis. They have, because of this, felt themselves obligated to justify the creation of public debt, not to understand and present the theory. They have sincerely considered that the citizenry must be saved from the orthodox fiscal norms that they held to be implicit in the classical analysis. To this group of scholars, macroeconomic policy aimed at providing full employment dictated the creation of public debt. Failure to issue debt might prolong unemployment of the nation's resources; hence, all arguments that suggest the cost side of debt become suspect. Yet, we may ask, why should public debt have been singled out for such a defensive reaction? Again, the source lies in the elementary confusion between debt and money creation, which becomes, in a slightly different sense, confusion between budget deficits and debt issue. If there is only one means of financing a budget deficit, namely, to issue public debt, then the fear that hard-headed analysis might foster unprincipled adherence to outmoded norms might be understandable, even if regrettable. But as we have already stressed, there is no logical connection between the creation of deficits in the budget and the financing of these deficits. For the financing, *debt creation and money creation are different instruments.*

Perhaps a majority of modern economists interprets the Keynesian lesson as follows: "In order to maintain high-level employment and growth, budgetary deficits are required. Deficits must be financed by borrowing. Therefore, public debt is desirable. Arguments that demonstrate that debt issue places a burden on future taxpayers must be vigorously opposed because their acceptance may reduce the public's willingness to undertake and pursue deficit spending."

In saying that this characterizes the attitude of many modern scholars, we shall, perhaps, be accused of caricature. But the statement does, we submit, more or less accurately describe the thought patterns of many who have contributed, in part unknowingly, to the analytical confusion.

Debt creation should not, of course, have been confused with deficit financing from the outset, at least for national governments with money-creating powers. If the objective is to shore up total demand in the economy, the optimal instrument for financing deficits is money creation. The confusion between money issue, which does not involve any shifting of cost forward in time, and debt issue, which does involve such a shifting, has persisted throughout the post-Keynesian discussion of fiscal policy. Even today, in 1966, this confusion is found in the writings of many sophisticated analysts.

Even if money creation is not, for any one of several reasons, a practicable alternative to debt issue, discussion of the effects of debt should never have got tangled up with fiscal policy norms. The fact that debt issue does place a cost on future taxpayers does not imply that debt should not be issued. In their zeal to dispel the prevailing pre-Keynesian wisdoms, modern scholars have too often bordered on the irresponsible.

Fortunately, this state of affairs seems on the way to correction. The excesses of zeal have largely passed, and the fallacies that now appear represent genuine confusion fostered by years of erroneous interpretation that has been passed along as received orthodoxy.

Conclusion

As economists, our primary concern is to insure that informed members of the political community think straight, and that confusion about the effects of alternative policy measures is dispelled. As economists, we cannot, and should not, recommend specific policies unless the objectives are clearly specified and widely accepted. This limited role of the economist remains highly important with respect to public debt. Confusion has reigned even over the elementary principles of public debt, and this confusion reached its peak during the late 1940s and early 1950s. Economists were primarily responsible through their failure to stick to analysis, and through their zeal to become social reformers. They should, in the late 1960s and the 1970s, accept the responsibility of setting the analytical record straight. Ideas once accepted are difficult to overthrow, however, even if these ideas can be demonstrated to be fallacious. Many ideas on public debt that now exist are of the latter stripe.

It is indeed fortunate that the ordinary man's conceptions of public debt have remained grounded in the elementary logic of debt itself. The policy excesses that might have been generated by a literal extension of the sophisticated fallacies of public debt were never realized. Hopefully, these fallacies are now on the way to slow and decent burial.

APPENDIX 1: A NOTE ON MEASUREMENT

Public debt is ordinarily measured by its maturity value. Using this measure, the national debt on June 30, 1965, was $317 billion. This, however, is not an adequate measure of the size of the debt because it does not tell us the amount of real resources that must be given up to discharge fully the obligation of the debt. Actually, somewhat less than $317 billion will discharge the obligation. In per capita terms, the maturity value of the public debt is about $1,600, and the problem of debt measurement is one of determining the per capita tax necessary to fully amortize the debt. This is somewhat less than $1,600 for two reasons. First, increases in interest rates enable repurchase of existing debts at below-maturity prices. Second, part of the debt represents disguised money creation and would not have to be retired.

Consider a debt instrument with a par value of $100 yielding $4 annual interest. If interest rates remain unchanged at 4 percent, $100 measures the size of the debt, for that is the amount which must be paid to repurchase the debt. What if the relevant interest rate rises to 5 percent? A $4 annual return would be a 5 percent return only if the value was $80. Thus a rise in the interest rate is equivalent to a fall in the capital value of the debt instrument. In this case the government should be able to repurchase the bond in the market for $80; $100 overstates the size of the public debt.

A second problem results from the fact that national debt, as it exists, is a mixture of debt and money. The presence of disguised money in the national debt is shown by the fact that the interest rate on the debt is significantly lower than the rate that would have to be paid on consols (perpetual debt). The rate paid on the public debt for the fiscal year ending June 30, 1965, was about 3.6 percent, whereas the yield on Moody's Aaa bonds, which is a good indication of the interest rate that would be necessary on pure debt, was 4.5 percent. The rate that the government would have to pay on consols would probably exceed the Moody's Aaa rate, so that 4.5 percent is a lower limit on what government bonds would yield if it were not for their moneyness. For illustrative purposes, assume $300 billion in national debt requires an interest rate of 3 percent ($9 billion annual interest payments). If the interest rate that would have to be paid on consols were 4 percent, then $9 billion annual payments would indicate a capital value of $225 billion. Only $225 billion of the $300 billion nominal public debt would be true debt, the remaining $75 billion would be disguised money creation. Debt retirement could take place with a $225 billion outlay, plus new money creation of $75 billion.

This simple conceptual apparatus may be used to give a rough estimate of the real value of the national debt as of June 30, 1965. In the first place, the $209 billion of marketable debt could be repurchased for 97 percent of its par value.[1] To make the calculation it can be assumed that nonmarketable securities also can be repurchased for 97 percent of their par values (except Savings Bonds which are carried in the current redemption values). In this manner the existing national debt could be repurchased for $308 billion instead of the $317 maturity value.

The market value of the national debt may now be segregated into real and monetized components. If the $11.5 billion annual interest charge is capitalized at 4.5 percent, the capital value of the debt is $225 billion. The remaining $53 billion of the market value (or $62 billion of maturity value) would represent the monetized portion of the national debt. If a 5 percent interest rate would have to be paid on consols, the capitalized value of the $11.5 billion interest payments would be $230 billion. In this case $78 billion of the market value would represent disguised money. Only $230 billion would be needed to retire the debt, or, stated differently, the economy would be unaffected if $230 billion of the national debt was refunded as consols at 5 percent interest while the remaining $78 billion was converted into money.

---

[1] These calculations are derived from the *Treasury Bulletin*, July, 1965, pp. 69-70.

This measure of national debt shows more adequately the burden of the debt than nominal maturity measures. That portion of the national debt which represents disguised money creation entails no burden; no exchange of purchasing power between citizens and the government was involved when the debt was created, so no reverse transfer from government to private citizens is required when it is retired.

APPENDIX 2: MATURITY STRUCTURE AND INTEREST CHARGES

The rise in interest charges that would result from a policy of funding is not so obvious as it may seem at first glance. Under normal conditions, the rate of interest will surely rise as the maturity structure lengthens, but as funding takes place the principal value of the debt may be reduced with no repercussions on the economy. A dollar's worth of debt with an average maturity structure of five years is equivalent to *less* than a dollar's worth of debt with a longer average maturity structure. To the extent that the shorter-term debt represents greater liquidity, that proportion need not be refunded. National debt serves both debt and liquidity purposes, with the proportion of liquidity increasing as the length of the debt decreases. Suppose a five-year bond represents $70 debt and $30 liquidity, and a consol represents $100 debt. Then a refunding of the $100 five-year bond could be done by issuing a $70 consol and creating $30 in money. Only the former requires interest payments. Now consider a ten-year bond that represents $80 debt and $20 liquidity. Refunding of the five-year bond would aim to maintain $30 in liquidity. A simple exchange for a $100 ten-year bond would reduce liquidity from $30 to $20. The proper refunding could take place by replacing the $100 five-year bond with an $87.50 ten-year bond and an increase of $12.50 in the money supply. Since the ten-year bond represents 20 percent liquidity, $70 of it is debt and $17.50 is liquidity. Thus the $100 five-year bond is equivalent to a $87.50 ten-year bond and an addition of $12.50 to the money supply; in

65

both cases there is $70 of debt and $30 of liquidity in the economy. As can be seen, interest charges need rise through funding only to the extent that the rate of increase in the interest rate as maturity lengthens exceeds the rate of decrease in liquidity as maturity lengthens. Some rise in interest charges seems likely if a funding policy is followed, but nothing like that indicated by a simple comparison of interest rates without considering that the principal values will differ.

SELECTED BIBLIOGRAPHY

H. C. Adams. 1893. *Public Debts.* New York: Appleton.

C. F. Bastable. 1895. *Public Finance,* 2nd ed. London: Macmillan.

James M. Buchanan. 1958. *Public Principles of Public Debt.* Homewood: Richard D. Irwin.

Colwyn Committee. 1927. *Report of the Committee on National Debt and Taxation.* London: H.M.Stationary Office.

Antonio De Viti De Marco. 1938. *First Principles of Public Finance.* Tr. by E. Marget. New York: Harcourt Brace.

James M. Ferguson, ed. 1964. *Public Debt and Future Generations.* Chapel Hill: North Carolina.

Tilford C. Gaines. 1962. *Techniques of Treasury Debt Management.* Glencoe: The Free Press.

Seymour E. Harris. 1947. *The National Debt and the New Economics.* New York: McGraw-Hill.

Abba P. Lerner. 1948. "The Burden of the National Debt." Pages 255-75 in *Income, Employment, and Public Policy.* New York: W. W. Norton.

OTHER AEI PUBLICATIONS

BOOKS

INTERNATIONAL PAYMENTS PROBLEMS (Symposium proceedings)—1966 ($7.00)

Papers:

The International Payments System: Postwar Trends and Prospects, *Gottfried Haberler*

Internal Policies Compatible with External Equilibrium at Stable Exchange Rates, *Friedrich A. Lutz*

Exchange-Rate Flexibility, *James E. Meade*

The International Payments System: Is There a Shortage of International Liquidity? *Roy L. Reierson*

International Monetary Systems and the Free Market Economy, *Fritz Machlup*

CONGRESS: THE FIRST BRANCH OF GOVERNMENT—1966 ($6.50)

Monographs:

Toward a New Model of Congress, *Alfred de Grazia*

"Check and Balance" Today: What Does It Mean for Congress and Congressmen? *Lewis Anthony Dexter*

Congress and the Executive: The Race for Representation, *Roger H. Davidson*

The Service Function of the United States Congress, *Kenneth G. Olson*

Congressional Liaison, *Edward de Grazia*

Introducing Radical Incrementalism into the Budget, *Aaron Wildavsky*

The Committees in a Revitalized Congress, *Heinz Eulau*

Decision Making in Congress, *James A. Robinson*

Legislative Oversight, *Cornelius P. Cotter*

Availability of Information for Congressional Operations, *Charles R. Dechert*

Information Systems for Congress, *Kenneth Janda*

Strengthening the First Branch: An Inventory of Proposals

Congress: 1989, *Alfred de Grazia*

STUDIES

Inflation: Its Causes and Cures, With a New Look at Inflation in 1966, *Gottfried Haberler*—1966

The U.S. Balance of Payments and International Monetary Reserves, *Howard S. Piquet*—1966 ($2.00)

The Federal Antitrust Laws, Revised Edition, *Jerrold G. Van Cise*—1965

The New United Nations—A Reappraisal of United States Policies, *George E. Taylor and Ben Cashman*—1965

French Planning, *Vera Lutz*—1965

70

The Free Society, *Clare E. Griffin*—1965, 138 pp. ($4.50)

Congress and the Federal Budget, *Murray L. Weidenbaum* and *John S. Saloma III*—1965, 209 pp. ($4.00)

Poverty: Definition and Perspective, *Rose D. Freidman*—1965

The Responsible Use of Power: A Critical Analysis of the Congressional Budget Process, *John S. Saloma III*—1964

Federal Budgeting—The Choice of Government Programs, *Murray L. Weidenbaum*—1964

The Rural Electrification Administration—An Evaluation, *John D. Garwood* and *W. C. Tuthill*—1963

The Economic Analysis of Labor Union Power, Revised Edition, *Edward H. Chamberlin*—1963

United States Aid to Yugoslavia and Poland—Analysis of a Controversy, *Milorad M. Drachkovitch*—1963

Communists in Coalition Governments, *Gerhart Niemeyer*—1963

Subsidized Food Consumption, *Don Paarlberg*—1963

Automation—The Impact of Technological Change, *Yale Brozen*—1963

Essay on Apportionment and Representative Government, *Alfred de Grazia*—1963 ($2.00)

American Foreign Aid Doctrines, *Edward C. Banfield*—1963

The Rescue of the Dollar, *Wilson E. Schmidt*—1963

The Role of Gold, *Arthur Kemp*—1963

Pricing Power and "Administrative" Inflation—Concepts, Facts and Policy Implications, *Henry W. Briefs*—1962

Depreciation Reform and Capital Replacement, *William T. Hogan*—1962

Consolidated Grants: A Means of Maintaining Fiscal Responsibility, *George C. S. Benson* and *Harold F. McClelland*—1961

The Patchwork History of Foreign Aid, *Lorna Morley* and *Felix Morley*—1961

U.S. Immigration Policy and World Population Problems, *Virgil Salera*—1960

Voluntary Health Insurance in the United States, *Rita R. Campbell* and *W. Glenn Campbell*—1960

*United States Aid and Indian Economic Development, *P. T. Bauer*—1959

Improving National Transportation Policy, *John H. Frederick*—1959

The Question of Governmental Oil Import Restrictions, *William H. Peterson*—1959

Labor Unions and the Concept of Public Service, *Roscoe Pound*—1959

Labor Unions and Public Policy, *Edward H. Chamberlin, Philip D. Bradley, Gerard D. Reilly,* and *Roscoe Pound*—1958, 177 pp. ($2.00)

National Aid to Higher Education, *George C. S. Benson* and *John M. Payne*—1958

Post-War West German and United Kingdom Recovery, *David McCord Wright*—1957

The Regulation of Natural Gas, *James W. McKie*—1957

Legal Immunities of Labor Unions, *Roscoe Pound*—1957

*Involuntary Participation in Unionism, *Philip D. Bradley*—1956

*The Role of Government in Developing Peaceful Uses of Atomic Energy, *Arthur Kemp*—1956

*The Role of The Federal Government in Housing, *Paul F. Wendt*—1956

*The Upper Colorado Reclamation Project, Pro by *Sen. Arthur V. Watkins,* Con by *Raymond Moley*—1956

Studies—$1.00 per copy unless otherwise indicated.

---

*Out of print.

LEGISLATIVE AND SPECIAL ANALYSES

89th Congress, First Session, 1965

The Appalachian Regional Development Bills. Bills by *Sen. Randolph; Rep. Fallon*

The Gold Cover Bill. Bills by *Sen. Robertson; Rep. Patman*

*Legislative History and Index of AEI Publications

Proposals to Provide Federal Aid to Elementary and Secondary Schools. Bills by *Sen. Morse; Rep. Perkins*

*Social Security Amendments of 1965. Bill by *Rep. Mills*

*Analysis of the Fiscal 1966 Federal Budget

*The Higher Education Bill of 1965. Bills by *Sen. Morse; Rep. Powell*

Housing and Urban Development Bills. Bills by *Sen. Sparkman* (by request); *Rep. Patman, Rep. Widnall*

*The Excise Tax Reduction Bill. Bill by *Rep. Mills*

*The Public Works and Economic Development Bill. Bill by *Sen. Douglas; Rep. Fallon*

To Create a Cabinet Department of Housing and Urban Development. Bill by *Rep. Fascell*

National Labor Policy. National High School Debate Series. *Special Analysis*

*Bills to Bar Enforcement of State Right-to-Work Laws. Bills by *Sen. McNamara; Rep. Thompson (N.J.), Rep. Griffin*

Proposed Federal Unemployment Compensation Legislation. Bills by *Sen. McCarthy; Rep. Mills, Rep. Byrnes*

History and Role of the National Labor Relations Board. *Special Analysis*

Crime and Law Enforcement. National College Debate Series. *Special Analysis* ($2.00)

---

*Out of print.

89th Congress, Second Session, 1966

*Legislative History, 89th Congress, 1st Session, and Index of AEI Publications

Proposals for 4-Year Term for Members of The House of Representatives

*Proposals for Revision of The Electoral College System

The Federal Budget for the 1967 Fiscal Year

Proposed Amendment to the Fair Labor Standards Act. Bill by *Rep. Dent*

The New Veterans' Benefits Law

The "Freedom of Information" Bill. Bill by *Sen. Long (Mo.)*

Proposed Federal Unemployment Compensation Legislation of 1966. A supplement to AEI 1965 Analysis

Housing and Urban Development Bills. Bills by *Sen. Sparkman; Rep. Patman*

The Water Pollution Control Bill. Bill by *Sen. Muskie*

The "Truth in Packaging" Bill. Bills by *Sen. Hart; Rep. Staggers*

The Bill to Suspend the Investment Tax Credit for Machinery and Equipment. Bill by *Rep. Mills*

Foreign Aid Policy of the United States. National High School Debate Series. *Special Analysis*

Foreign Policy Commitments of the United States. National College Debate Series. *Special Analysis* ($2.00)